AF541249

IMPACT OF MICRO-FINANCE THROUGH SELF-HELP GROUPS

IMPACT OF MICRO-FINANCE THROUGH SELF-HELP GROUPS

By

Dr. R.M. Patil

M.Com., LL.B., Ph.D.

Associate Professor

Department of Commerce,

G. P. Porwal Arts, Commerce &

V. V. Salimath Science College

Sindgi - 586 128 (Karnataka)

(INDIA)

DPH

DISCOVERY PUBLISHING HOUSE PVT. LTD.

NEW DELHI-110 002

Published by:
Tilak Wasan

DISCOVERY PUBLISHING HOUSE PVT. LTD.
4383/4B, Ansari Road, Darya Ganj
New Delhi-110 002 (India)
Phone : +91-11-23279245, 43596064-65
Fax : +91-11-23253475
E-mail : discoverypublishinghouse@gmail.com
sales@discoverypublishinggroup.com
parul.wasan@gmail.com
web : www.discoverypublishinggroup.com

***First Edition:* 2014**

ISBN: 978-93-5056-486-8

Impact of Micro-finance through Self-help Groups

Printed at:
Dynamic Printers
Delhi

PREFACE

Micro-financing through SHGs could benefit overall society by overcoming the liquidity. It generates benefits to only that portion of the poor that is able to use loan for income-generating activities. Borrowing will increase their income and sustain self-employment. The post independence era in the country has seen a series of policy interventions for assuring an effective institutional arrangement for meeting the financial needs of the society. The Banks were nationalized, directed lending by way of insisting the financial institutions for lending to priority sectors, NABARD established poverty alleviation programmes were launched and economic reforms were introduced by the government to uplift and empower the rural poor especially the women. But, were not enough to tackle the problem of poverty and at the same time subsidy linked government programmes could not prove effective, because of the huge member households, limited resources, inadequacies in the implementation, huge implementation cost, leakages etc. The NABARD's experiment proved successful as the poor people could successfully access credit from formal credit system. This paved way for launching of pilot projects of forming 255 SHGs and credit linking them with banks. The implementation of the pilot project was an instant success. Southern states including Karnataka were in the forefront. This, SHG Bank Linkage Programme has been the most successful poverty alleviation programme so far. More them 69 Lakh SHG were linked to Bank by the end of March 2010. This clearly shows that the poor especially women in India particularly in Karnataka are benefited by this programme. All these developments have made a socio-economic impact on the members of the SHGs.

Number of distinguished scholars helped me in the completion of this book. Without their help this book would not have been completed. I profusely thank all. My sincere thanks are due to my esteemed colleagues for their encouragement and acknowledge the encouragement extended to me by Shri. B. M. Biradar Retired Principal, G. P. Porwal College, Sindgi.

I am very much thankful to NABARD officials, bank managers and the staff of various bank branches, and SHG members of this region who provided me all the information needed for completion of the Study.

I am indebted to my father Shri. M. K. Patil without whose blessings, I could not have come up to this higher learning. I owe a sense of gratitude to my friend Shri J. S. Pujari, Adult Education Officer, Bijapur district, Shri R. V. Jalawadi, Associate Professor, S. K. College, Talikoti, Shri S. T. Dhanode, Associate Professor, S. P. M. Arts and Commerce College, Raibag, Shri S. O. Halasagi, Associate Professor, Shivanand College, Kagawad and other friends for their constant encouragement and support throughout my career.

I thank my wife Smt. Shailaja too for her heart-felt support in completing this study. I recollect with a deep sense of affection, the love showered upon me by my son Vivek and daughter Vasudha.

Author

CONTENTS

ABBREVIATIONS

SHG	:	Self-help Group
NABARD	:	National Bank for Agriculture and Rural Development
MFI	:	Micro-finance Institution
SHPA	:	Self-help Promoting Agency
SHPI	:	Self-help Promoting Institution
SGSY	:	Swarnajayanti Gram Swarojagar Yojana
SBLP	:	Self-help Group Bank-Linkage Programme
RRBs	:	Regional Rural Banks
RF	:	Revolving Fund
MF	:	Micro-finance
PLR	:	Prime Lending Rate
MFO	:	Micro-finance Organization
MYRAD	:	Mysore Resettlement and Development Agency
IRDP	:	Integrated Rural Development Programme
GDP	:	Gross Domestic Product
BRI	:	Bank Rakyat Indonesia
BRAC	:	Bangladesh Rural Advancement Committee
BPL	:	Below Poverty Line
NGOs	:	Non-Government Organizations
RBI	:	Reserve Bank of India
PACB	:	Primary Agricultural Co-operative Bank

DRDA	:	District Rural Development Agency
RMK	:	Rastreeya Mahisla Kosh
JLG	:	Joint Liability Group
SKDRDP	:	Shri Kshetra Dharmasthala Rural Development Programme
WCDC	:	Women and Child Development Department
SKS	:	Swayam Krishi Sangham
SIDBI	:	Small Industries Development Bank of India
IASC	:	Indian Association of Savings and Credit
PSCB	:	Pustikar Samiti Co-operative Credit Bank
CSWB	:	Central Social Works Board
WWF	:	Working Women's Forum
SEWA	:	Self-Employed Women's Association
CDF	:	Co-operative Development Foundation
WDP	:	Women's Development Programme
RAS	:	Rayalseema Seva Samiti
YCO	:	Youth Charitable Organization
UMSV	:	Utkal Mahila Sanchaya Vikas
PREM	:	People Rural Education Movement
NBFCs	:	Non-Banking Finance Companies
BASIX	:	Bharatiya Samrudhi Investments and Consulting Services
SHARE	:	Society for Helping Awakening Rural Poor through Education

INTRODUCTION

Poverty alleviation has been an important issue before the developing nations of the world. This is a great challenge for the South Asian Countries, as about half of the world's poor live in this region. The intensity of poverty is high in India. The poverty ratio is 28 per cent which subsist on less then US $1 a day. Moreover the problem is more acute in rural sector. The Indian development planning has not been able to bring about an appreciable change in India's traditional social and economic structure. The provision in the Indian constitution that every citizen has a right to earn livelihood and that the state shall direct its policies towards achieving this goal, has hardly been of any use to those living in the remote rural areas in a state of misery, social and economic backwardness, ignorance and helplessness. It is well known that the gap between the rich and the poor has widened over the years. No doubt, development has taken place throughout the country but in reality the people groveling in poverty have been passed under the planned development.

Since independence, the Government of India has experimented with a large number of subsidy based community and wage based poverty alleviation programmes. But these programmes have not been able to successfully meeting the social and economic objectives of poverty reduction. Much of this failure was due to a lack of involvement by the people during any stage of the implementation of the programmes.

Poverty in India has predominantly been a rural character. While there are several structural dimensions to the rural poverty, it is generally accepted that it rises due to the lack of capital or lack of surplus. The rural poor are in perpetual poverty and victims of the 'vicious cycle of poverty'. Therefore, the established policy prescription tries to break this cycle of poverty through infusion of credit. Hence credit is the major policy thrust for rural poverty alleviation. Micro-finance programmes have, in recent past, become one of the more promising ways to used scarce development funds to achieve the objectives of poverty alleviation. Micro-finance is recognised as a key strategy for addressing issues of poverty alleviation and women empowerment. Access to financial services and subsequent transfer of funds, financial resources to the poor enable them to become economic agents of change.

Micro-finance is a noble and holistic approach of banking with poor with the distinct advantage of high repayments of loan and low transaction cost. Micro-finance is distinctly different from other poverty alleviation schemes. Loans under micro-finance programmes are very small, on an average less than US $ 100 by world standards and in hundreds of rupees by Indian standards. Micro-finance continues to target the rural and urban households with emphasis on women borrowers, provision of finance for creation of income-generating and their maintenance and bringing greater quality of services.

Role of micro-finance in eradication of poverty has been stressed by the United Nations in its Economic and Social Council meet on July 25, 1997 in which the council called for strengthening the micro-credit institutions. Also it recognised the importance of access to credit of the people living below poverty line to develop farm sector and to undertake micro-enterprises to generate self-employment. UN while declaring the year 2005 as the International year of Micro-finance has focused on many issues concerning micro-finance.

India has been experimenting with micro-finance strategy in the form of Self-Help Groups (SHGs) as a part of formal credit delivery system since 1960s, giving lot of freedom to Non-Government Organizations (NGOs) to set-up SHGs on various models. Micro-credit through SHG's becomes a ladder for the poor to bring them economically but also socially, mentally, and physically sound. Governments of India and the Reserve Bank of India, realising the importance of micro-credit in the development programme have taken up the many steps for the linkage of the SHGs with formal financial institutions. The basic purpose of the linkage is to strengthen the financial health of SHGs by ensuring adequate flow of bank credit to these institutions.

MICRO-CREDIT HISTORICAL PERSPECTIVE

Micro-finance, as a tool of empowerment of the poor has been adopted in other developing countries. Grameen Bank experiment in Bangladesh indicates that by adopting certain innovative practices. It has been possible to target the beneficiaries to a fair extant. Linking the Banking institutions with the help of SHGs in mobilizing rural savings for meeting the credit needs of the rural areas was recommended in 1986 in the 6th General Assembly of Asia and Pacific Regional Agricultural Credit Association held at Kathmandu, Nepal.

Subsequently in 1988-89 at National Bank for Agriculture and Rural development (NABARD) conducted a study of ORGOs and based on findings, launched pilot project in 1992 for assisting 500 SHGs through commercial banks. Accordingly 225 SHGs were linked with banks during 1992-93 as an indicator of a modest beginning of micro-finance in India. By the end of March 2001, about 2.63 lakh groups have been covered under the programme. It has been found that this system has several merits namely near cent per cent recovery, low transaction cost, monitoring being easy and less time consuming. This has also strengthened saving habits among group members.

Rastriya Mahila Kosh (RMK) was set-up under the ages of the Department of Women and Child Development in March 1993 took up provision of micro-finance with particular focus on the women groups. The Kosh has assisted 939 SHGs covering over 9.13 lakh women and provided Rs. 106.05 crore as loan so far.

THE CONCEPT OF MICRO-FINANCE

The term micro-finance is of recent origin and is commonly used while discussing issues relating to poverty alleviation intervention, income distribution among a wider section of population, savings in small amounts and small loans. The affordability, availability and accessibility of small loans in a flexible, sensitive and responsive manner, the availability of timely, adequate and un-interrupted finance to those who cannot provide collateral security in a non-bureaucratically style. The term micro literally means 'Small'. But the task force has not defined any amount. However as per the micro-credit special cell of the RBI the borrowers accounts up to the limit of Rs. 25,000 could be considered as micro-credit products and this amount could be gradually increased up to Rs. 40,000 over a period of time which roughly equal to US $500 – a standard for south Asia. As per international perceptions the term micro-finance, sometimes is used inter changeably with the term micro-credit. However, while micro-credit refers to purveyed of loans in small quantities, the term micro-finance has a broader meaning covering in its ambit, other financial services like, savings, insurance etc. Micro-finance comprises a set of services used as a sustainable tool to combat poverty. The set of activities and services of Micro-finance are as follows:

- Micro-credit and loans primarily for income-generation activities.
- Micro-savings or small savings on borrower's own resources.

Features of Micro-finance

The important features of micro-finances are as follows:

- It is a tool for empowerment of the poorest.
- The micro-credit is delivered normally through self-help groups.
- It is essentially for promoting self-empowerment and productivity in informal sector of economy.
- It is generally used for direct income-generation and consumption smoothing.
- It is not just a financing system but a tool for social and economic charge, especially for women.
- It provides for seasonality, allow repayment flexibility, and avoid bureaucratic and legal formalities.

- It assists the women to perform traditional roles better and to take up micro-entrepreneurship.

SOCIO-ECONOMIC IMPACT OF MICRO-FINANCE

Micro-finance programmes enable the members to save and set-up and expand a credit fund consisting of savings and/or resources mobilizing from donors/banks, so that members can initiate income-generating activities. It also enables the member households to acquire productive assets such as: livestock, land, etc. The socio-economic impacts of the members of the SHGs are as follows:

- Income of the SHG members would increase.
- The direct access to credit would bring a long-term economic improvement of the household.
- Increase in income of the household would induce higher expenditure on food, clothing, health and education etc.
- Increase in income would reflect improvement in the standard of living.
- Better education to their children.
- Social status of the members especially women in the village as well as at home would increase.
- Enables the member to get banking awareness and awareness about the government.
- Active involvement of members in socio-economic and political activities.

Socio-economic Transformation

- The members of the SHGs are approaching banks. The interaction with the bankers has made them to learn many things.
- Members of the group would attain functional literacy status.
- Members have a say in the important family decisions.
- Status in the village and family would be increased.
- The possession of the household articles would be increased.
- Women could able to spend money in emergencies.
- Enables the members of provide better education to their children.

MICRO-FINANCE INTERNATIONAL EXPERIENCES

Micro-finance industry, which began in 1976 with the establishment of Grameen Bank in Bangladesh, is now worldwide movement comprising thousands of specialist banks, credit unions, co-operatives, village credit societies, NGOs and charities spanning both the richest and poorest countries. Their basic purpose is to extend the outreach of banking services, especially business credit, to those who do not qualify for normal bank loan.

In some countries, with the maturing of micro-finance industry, MFIs have established associations or interest groups to initiate formalization process. They have initiated a dialogue with regulators and policy makers to define the appropriate regulatory approach for their environment and supporting the initiative, they built up databases, defined best practices and specified industry standards though the adoption of industry standards in voluntary. Many Southeast Asian and Latin American countries have been implemented the micro-finance programmes.

Bangladesh

Since 1985-86 poverty had risen consistently in the country due to rapid increase in the working age population, increasing landlessness and low growth of employment in non-farm sector. According to the Bangladesh Bureau of Statistics Sources, 47.5 per cent of the population in 1991-92 lived below poverty line, paged to daily intake of 2122 calories. The incidence of poverty was broadly similar both in rural and urban areas. Jha (2002), concluded in his paper on micro-finance models in Bangladesh, despite a few weakness, demonstrated a number of strong positive attribute in terms of operational simplicities, better accessibilities wider outreaches, emphasis on women empowerment and availability of a wide range of financial and non-financial services.

Rural credit in Bangladesh is provided by three different types of institutions as formal, semi-formal and informal credit agencies. Formal agencies include agricultural banks, rural branches of Nationalized Commercial Banks, Grameen Banks, two Co-operative networks and private banks. The semi-formal agencies include Non-Governmental Organizations (NGOs). The informal sector consists of private money lenders, friends, relatives, shop-keepers, etc.

Grameen Bank is the largest provider of micro-credit in Bangladesh. After liberation of the country in 1971, Prof. Mohd Yunus, the man behind the grameen bank, realised that getting credit from the banking system without collateral was an impossible task for the poor, who were in dire need of it, and the money lenders were exploiting the poor beyond imagination. Therefore, he obtained certain amount from the bank for on lending without any security/collateral to the poor who were organized into small groups. Prof. Yunus started the experiment in Chittagong district in 1976 by giving small amounts to the borrowers to buy raw materials like bamboo etc. After selling goods, they repaid the money. The process was repeated again and again and the institution promoted by Prof. Yunus in 1976 and expanded its operations to other districts of Bangladesh.

The bank was constituted under Grameen Bank Ordinance of the Government of Bangladesh in 1983. The bank lends without any collateral security to groups and a group consists of five members coming from different families. There is no membership fee and savings is not compulsory for access to loan in first instance. Saving starts after the first loan, when repayment starts in weekly installments, members can avail of loans any number of times after repaying earlier loans, which are generally repayable in 50 weekly installments, excepting housing loans, which has a repayment starts period of three years. Loans are given for processing and manufacturing, agriculture and forestry, livestock and fisheries, service activities, trading, peddling, shop-keeping, housing, seasonal loans for cultivation, cattle rearing, leasing, equipment leasing, medium size loans and education loans for member's children. The loans carry interest rates ranging between 5 to 20 per cent per annum. Repayment installments consist of principal, interest and compulsory deposit of the borrowers.

The Bangladesh Rural Advancement Committee (BRAC) was established in 1972, initially, with an aim to provide relief and rehabilitation to the refugees. It shifted its emphasis in 1973 to community development involving the rural poor. In 1976, it adopted a target group approach consisting of the landless and the poorest, particularly the women. It has also decided to discontinue taking donor funds and to make itself sustainable by 2001. The aim of BRAC is to help the poor, who are willing to embark on activities to better their lives, through its savings and credit programme.

Indonesia

The record of poverty alleviation in Indonesia has been remarkable since 1975. The poverty reduction level in Indonesia was possible due mainly to the achievement of rapid economic growth, the implementation of financial sector reforms from 1980 onwards and the initiatives taken by the government for focusing on poverty ranged from 1.3 per cent in Jakarta to 46 per cent in the West Nusa Tanggara Vulnerabilities to poverty remain considerable given the large number of households just above the poverty line.

Nepal

Nepal is one of the poorest countries in the world with an estimated 42 per cent of the population below the poverty line Rs. 4500. While poverty in urban areas, is less pronounced of 23 per cent in the rural areas, where 90 per cent of the population live. Poverty is estimated at 44 per cent. The country like India, has adopted a system of planned development under which development plans are prepared (five year plans) and implemented towards alleviating poverty suffered from poor implementation and failed to achieve their objectives, resulting in an increase in the number of poor people in the country.

Philippines

In Philippines, a family of five having an income below 7400 Pesos per month is considered to be poor while a family with an income up to 1000 Pesos is categorised as the poorest of the poor. Among the South East Asian Countries, the incidence of poverty, particularly in the rural areas, is substantially higher in the country. Poverty in rural areas is attributed to lack of access of the poor to financial resources provided by formal credit institutions. The year 1980 witnessed changes in the policies and programme is to tackle poverty in the country. One of the major policy changes was, involving the government banks in the wholesale lending to the private banks. These changes in the policies were a reflection of the commitment of the government to provide essential credit facilities to the poor, who did not have any access in the past.

Thailand

Thailand had the largest proportional reduction in poverty between 1975 and 1995. The concept of micro-finance as perceived by the banking sector in Thailand distinctly differs from the Asian countries, especially India. There is no specific definition of micro-finance or micro-credit in the country. There are rather a large number of tiny enterprises with the household participating in running them. In the area of micro-finance, the Government is the leading player providing support for community development and improving the employment opportunities in the country through various programmes (Antic T. M. and Watson). However, these programmes cover not only poor but also those who are not so poor but need credit.

Sri Lanka

Micro-finance in Sri Lanka has and credit co-operatives in 1911 with the enactment of the Co-operative Credit Societies Ordinance. The sector grew most rapidly during the last 20 years when micro-finance, as an instrument to reduce poverty, gained the attention and support of both the Government and funding agencies. The Bank of Ceylon, inaugurated in 1938, and the People's Bank established in 1961, was set-up to provide financial services to smaller borrowers and rural people (Dulan De Silva).

LATIN AMERICAN COUNTRIES

The two major economic crises in the last 15 years, having its origin in Mexico had its impact on the poverty levels in many of the Latin American countries. As a result of Mexico's debt crisis in the 1980s, Poverty levels increased by more than 30 per cent in Argentina and Mexico while the crisis of 1995-96 had resulted in an increase in poverty by more than 50 per cent (Lusting N. and Walton M., 1998). The governments in these countries had responded with initiating a variety of programmes to tackle the issue of rising poverty.

Argentina

In Argentina, around 85 per cent of total population (33 million) lives in urban areas while 11 million people live in the Metropolitan region. The country significantly reduced poverty in the early 1990s compared to the immediately preceding years as a result of successful micro-economic stabilization programme. Increasing income-generating opportunities through sustained economic growth and boosting investment in women capital facilitated reduction in the poverty levels in the country.

Bolivia

The poverty report of Bolivia has traced some progress in reducing urban poverty between 1976 and 1992; little has been achieved in rural areas of the country, having a high concentration of the poor generally, poor are wage earners. Who have limited land holdings and lack access to credit and basic infrastructure. Two apex organizations, PRODEM and Banco Sol are providing micro-finance to the poor as a bank promoted by the former PRODEM founded in 1986, by the group of Bolivian business leaders with assistance from ACCION international for introducing financial services in the rural and urban areas in the country and for increasing access to credit for the poor. In 1998 PRODEM had 47,130 active clients, included merchants producers and service providers. The loan amount disbursed by the organization during the period 1994 to 1998 was 44 million US $ (Chen G. 1997).

Chillie

According to the poverty assessment summary for Chillie, even within a short period of time (1987-94), there has been a significant decline in poverty. The poverty head count and poverty deficit was halved during this period. Poverty declined from 41 per cent in 1987 to 23 per cent by 1994. Chilies' success in reducing poverty between 1987 and 1994 compares favorably with countries such as China, Indonesia and Korea. PROPESA, an organization founded in 1988 by a group of Chilean businessmen with support from ACCION International, is dedicated to creating jobs and bettering the lives of micro-entrepreneurs in the informal sector through credit programme and training. Start up and operational funding for the organization came primarily from USAID while the portfolio was capitalized with loans from the domestic banks, which were backed by ACCION's Latin American Bridge fund. The clients of PROPESA are involved in a variety of commercial activities such as cloth manufacturing, carpentry and appliance repairs. About 80 per cent of its clients are engaged in manufacturing while 10 per cent are involved in commerce and a small percentage is service providers. The organization has disbursed loans totaling US $ 36 million during the period 1994-98 and an amount of US $ 3.8 million disbursed to 3828 clients was active during 1998.

Colombia

Poverty in the country declined steadily from an estimated 50 per cent of the population in 1964 to 9 per cent in 1992. Nevertheless, disparities in income and living standards continue among regions and socio-economic groups.

The four important micro-finance institutions operating in Colombia are the Actuar Tolima, Co-operative Expender, Fundacion Mario Santa Domingo (FMSD) and Finamerica. Actuar Tolima was established in 1986 to help victims of a devastating mudslide rebuild their lives and communities. It is affiliated to ACCION's Latin American network since 1996. By 1998, the organization had loaned over US $ 37 million to 21000 micro-entrepreneurs, of whom more than 50 per cent were women.

CURRENT INDIAN SOCIO-ECONOMIC SCENARIO

The socio-economic landscape of India has undergone tremendous changes, with visible signs of growth momentum in all sectors. However growth per se is not sustainable, unless the benefits of growth are wide spread. While Indian economy has shown an average growth of 9 per cent in the last three years, the benefits have not equitably percolated to the different segments of our economy especially to those in the lower rungs in the social economic ladder thus negating the trickledown theory of growth. The rural agriculture sector in particular has not gained the desired momentum of growth and development. Nevertheless the high growth has raised expectation of the people for better delivery of core public services. These expectations, if left unmet, will result in social disorder due to the prevalent social disparity. Therefore, there is an urgent need for empowering and creating opportunities for each person.

Despite spending enormous sums the government has failed dismally to provide every village with the five basics of growth-all weather roads, electricity, telephone, functioning schools, and functioning health centres. Huge sums have been spent on employment programmes, which were supposed to create durable rural assets. This has not happened because of the fact that good infrastructure cannot be created through labour intensive means instead; we need mechanized, capital intensive approaches to poverty alleviation. The attitude of the government to subsidies and services has made the situation worse. Providing free electricity and water to the rural sector encourage excessive pumping that dries up all the drinking water wells and allow all shallow tube wells of middle peasants leaving water only for the deep tube wells of the rich. Free canal water has encouraged water guzzling crops that are ecologically in appropriate. Education and health services provided by the staff belong to trade unions with huge political clout. In India everything is in a mess. There is no proper planning. If there is planning, there is no co-ordination.

DELIVERY MODELS OF MICRO-FINANCE OPERATING IN INDIA

Micro-finance network in India has the largest financial network in the world. Four different of Micro-finance models are operating in India. Among these self-group model is more popular way of approaching the poor especially women.

(i) Self Help Group – Model

SHGs are working in India as a port of formal credit delivery system since statistics giving lot of. If scope for the development of not government organizations. The SHGs have recognising the importance of micro-credit the Government of India and the RBI have taken among steps for the linkage of SHGs with banks and financial institutions. The objective of linkage is to strengthen the financial health of SHGs by ensuring adequate flow of bank credit to these institutions.

NABARD is playing an important role in the growth of SHGs in India. SHG model is performing well in India in providing credit support to the poor. SHGs the major form of delivery of micro-credit have made a revolutionary changes in the lives of lakhs of rural poor especially women.

The SHGs in India are formed under any MFIs and NGOs, MFIs are also playing crucial role in uplifting the economic conditions of the asset less poor.

SHG is a small voluntary organization of the poor people having 10-20 members preferably from the same economic background. They came together for solving their common problems through mutual help. SHGs promotes the habit of savings and helps in building up strong common fund and have the accumulated sizeable fund to meet the emergent needs of their members the building consumption needs.

(ii) Grameen Model

Grameen Bank is the largest provider of micro-credit in Bangladesh. Prof. Mohd. Yunus, started experiment in Chittagong district in 1976 by giving small amounts to the borrowers to buy raw materials like bamboo under this system a bank unit is set us covering an area of 15-20 villages under this model for member get loan without any collateral security and there is no membership fees and saving is not compulsory for access to loan in first in fence. Sing starts after the first loan, when repayment starts in weekly installments, member can avail loans any number of times after repaying earlier loans, which are generally repayable in so weekly installments except housing loans, which has a repayment period of three years. This Model is not popular in India Swayam Krishi Sangham (SKS); in Uttar Pradesh are examples of this model in India.

(iii) Mixed Model

This model is the combination of self-help group and grameen model. BASI and Indian association of savings and credit (IASC) are the examples for mixed model in India.

(iv) Individual Banking Model

Under this model micro loans are given directly to the borrower. Formation of group is not necessary under this model. Pustikar Samiti Co-operative Banking (PSCB) in Jodhpur, Rajasthan follows this method of lending asset less poor individually.

Among these models SHGs model is best suited to India and dominated as a delivery channel of micro-finance.

ROLE OF NGOs IN PROMOTING SHGs

In India NGOs are playing significant role in development programmes. Recognising the importance of NGOs, the planners in the first five-year plan the central social work Board (CSWB) was set-up in 1953. The main function of this board was to provide financial assistance to voluntary organizations in order to develop them (Bhatia). The active involvement was started only after the seventh plan. NGOs involvement in women empowerment through group based was started in 1980. Today there are large numbers of NGOs that have undertaken the task of financial intermediaries. The 9th 5 year plan envisaged the involvement of NGOs right from the planning process. Under Swarna Jayanthi Gram Swarojagar Yojana (SGSY) Scheme since 1994, group lending remained the major thrust for the government as a part of poverty alleviation. Since NGO have already done pioneering work in SHG promotion, they are being extensively involved in influencing the SHGs (Bose, 2003).

Some of the women's NGOs who have taken initiatives in the field were Co-operative Development Foundation (IDF), Andhra Pradesh; Working Women's Forum (WWF), Tamil Nadu; Self-Employed Women's Association (SEWA), Gujarat; and Women's Development Programme (WDP), Rajasthan. Besides the above NGOs there were others like the Mysore Resettlement and Development Agency (MYRADA), in Karnataka, PRADAN in Tamil Nadu, the Royalseema Seva Samithi (RAS) and Youth Charitable Organization (YCO) in Andhra Predesh, the Utkal Mahila Sanchaya Vikas (UMSU) under the ages of People Rural Education Movement (PREM), the Gram Vikas in Orissa, etc.

There are several other NGOs which followed suit throughout the country (Jayasheela, Shriprasad H. and Dinesh P. T., 2009).

The emerging model of intervention of majority of NGOs working in rural areas is the SHG group model of micro-finance pioneered by MYRADA in the late 1970s in Karnataka since them most of the NGOs in South India and many NGOs from North too have started this model in undertaking many of their developmental activities. (Jayasheela, Shriprasad H., Dinesh P. T., opp. cit.)

Chandrakavate (2003) opines that the programme of micro-financing through SHGs with the introduction of NGOs and support from government has shown many positive impacts on rural poor women. Thus NGOs have popularized the concept of micro-finance in India.

MICRO-FINANCE INSTITUTIONS

Micro-finance institution acts as an interface between the formal credit delivery institutions and credit sackers with an aim to assist for the socio-economic development of the poor and marginalized people (Jayasheela, Shriprasad H and Dinesh P. T (2009). MFI's in India are playing crucial role in uplifting the assets poor. They are growing rapidly and are highly efficient in India Three categories of MFIs are providing financial services. They are:

- *Not for Profit MFIs;* They are working similar to Grameen Bank Style.
- *Mutual Benefit MFIs*; These are usually Co-operatives working on co-operative principles.
- *For Profit MFIs*; These incorporated as NBFCs such as BASIX and SHARE micro-finance ltd. Various government and private sector institutions offering micro-finance services in India. NABARD, SIDBI and RMK are the government institutions. Providing micro-finance services, besides commercial banks, regional Rural Banks (RRBs) and co-operative bank are also rendering the services to the poor. The MFIs are mainly in the private sector.

Over the years the micro-finance sector has been a continued expansion of the SHG-Bank linkage programme along with under regional spread, increased innovation and outreach of MFIs rapidly increasing micro-finance portfolios of commercial banks, development of products for insurance and pension scale ups is partnership between commercial banks and MFIs (Tan Kha etc. 2005).

THE CONCEPT OF SELF-HELP GROUPS

Self-Help Group (SHG) is a group of like minded people who come together to pool their small to a common fund and agree to meet their emergency need on mutual help basis. The group decides whom the loan should be given to, for which purpose, on what terms and at what schedule of recovery. The focus of decision making is shifted to the group, which provides the members with the opportunity to develop the skill to negotiate, to decide on what is manageable and feasible, to impose sanctions where required and to adjust repayment schedules if circumstances makes the previously agreed to schedule impossible to follow (Fernandez 2007). The provision of credit is therefore not the only objective; more important to develop the members skill to manage finance. Collective wisdom and peer pressure of group members help in proper use as well as timely repayment of credit.

Features of SHGs

The following are the features of SHGs:

- 10-20 persons having similar socio-economic background from SHG's.
- SHGs are informal groups register themselves under the Societies Registration Act, the State Co-operative Act, or a Partnership Firm Act.
- Each SHG has its own written by-laws regarding savings, rate of interest, repayment period, meetings etc.
- Group leaders are elected by members and rotated periodically.
- Inter lending brings immediately for a verity of small needs.
- Group members usually create a common fund by contributing their small savings on a regular basis.
- Once the group shows its performance maturity, it is linked to the local rural bank branch.
- The group can apply to the bank for loans within 6 months of opening the bank account.
- The group takes loans from the bank at a fixed interest without any collateral securities.
- The group on-lends to its members with flexible repayment schedule and the rate of interest, which is decided by the group.
- The group takes the responsibility of timely repayment to the bank, even if the members are in default because of an emergency.
- Participatory decision-making.
- Traditional and non-traditional production and consumption.
- Transparency in operation.
- Simple documentation.
- Flexible and responsive.

- Mutual Confidence and trust.
- Group solidarity, self-help, awareness, social and economic empowerment.

Grading of SHGs

Grading is a necessary process done through a grading exercise to test whether the group has evolved in to a good group and is ready to get into the next stage of evolution. This enables the banks to establish linkages with good groups. The first grading has to be done after six months of the formation of the SHGs to ensure bank-linkage of successful groups and making revolving fund available to them. The groups are graded on the basis of parameters such as size of the SHG, saving capacity, meeting and attendance, tendency of loan seeking and repayment, and record maintenance. Ever quarter grading exercise ought to be taken till such time all the groups obtain good grade.

SHGs and Revolving Fund

Revolving fund is seed capitals in the form of grant or interest free loan provided by the SHPI/DRDA to supplement the resources of the SHGs. It can be formed through membership fee, interest earned on saving, and loan of the members or by aid from the bank/ external agencies, and penalty etc. DRDA provides the revolving fund to those groups out of the 10 per cent of SGSY – revolving fund, who have been in existence for a period of six months and demonstrate the potential of a sizable group.

Origin of the Research Problem

Micro-finance has emerged as a needful programme to cater to the needs of the most under privileged people *i.e.,* tribal, dalits and women. The major concern today is ever increasing poverty and there is urgent need of empowering, enabling the most neglected sections of the society through organized support to all poverty alleviation programmes. Considering the paucity of funds with poor people, the need of the hour is to provide adequate credit to the needy people to enable them to undertake entrepreneurial activity, however small, with the help of NGOs and GOs. Micro-finance is expected to play pivotal role in poverty eradication and employment generation.

Belgaum division of Karnataka State comprises 7 Districts, 49 Talukas and all the Talukas are grouped in the category of most/more backward and backward areas as per Dr. Nanjunadappa Committee Report. The committee was appointed by the Government of Karnataka to study the regional imbalance in the state of Karnataka. Out of the total population 67 per cent stays in rural areas and 38 per cent are in below poverty line. Though, the region includes many numbers of commercial banks, co-operative banks, and regional rural bank branches the existing branch network is insufficient to address the requirements of the growing population. Studies reveal that rural credit has come down drastically in recent years. Provision of Micro-finance as a response to the requirement of the region and to the policy initiative of government of India to develop the rural areas was started in this region with slow footing. With the launching of SHG-Bank Linkage Programme (SBLP) by NABARD and Swarna Jayanti Gram Swarozagar Yojana (SGSY) scheme of employment creation by GOI, group formation and their linkage were accelerated. Self-help groups bank-linkage programme is a socio-economic programme. Different agencies *i.e.,* the government and government organizations, non-government organizations, financial institutions etc., have been involved in implementation of this programme. This movement has a considerable impact on socio-economic life of the members. Against this background, the present study has been undertaken.

SIGNIFICANCE OF THE STUDY

Micro-finance programme appeared as an essential tool in reducing poverty. This subject has gained a considerable significance in the recent past as an area of policy interventions and initiatives. However, this consideration is absent in most of the real situation especially where deprivation and backwardness prevail in this region has been categorised as most/more backward and backward areas as per Dr. Nanjudappa Committee Report in recent years. Therefore, the present study has been undertaken to find out whether SHGs are really helpful in eradicating poverty of poor members. Hence, the study has been undertaken.

Objectives

The principal objectives of the study are:

1. To study the impact of SHGs Bank-linkage programme on socio-economic status of the members of the group.
2. To study whether the SHGs are instrumental in enhancing economic and social status of the members.
3. To study the extent of mobilization of funds and generation of income by the SHGs.
4. To ascertain the problems before SHGs.
5. To offer suggestions to overcome the problems before SHGs.

METHODOLOGY

The study is based on both types of data *i.e.,* primary and secondary data. Primary data will be collected through well structured questionnaires, and party interview. The secondary data will be collected from books, journals and related reports. The study is based on the sample selection of SHGs from each district. Convenient sampling method has been adopted to select the sample size. Tools like percentages, simple averages are used in order to analyse the data. The present study is limited to Belgaum division of Karnataka state. 12,531 SHG members, 901 SHGs and 350 banks spread over 7 districts and 49 talukas are selected for the study.

DATA COLLECTION

Two separate questionnaires are used for data collection. Questionnaire – I is used for collecting data relating to SHG member while Questionnaire – II is used for ascertaining data from the banks. In addition to this secondary data are obtained from NABARD reports, books, Journals and thesis.

TOOLS OF ANALYSIS

Various statistical tools are employed for analysing the data. Simple techniques like averages and percentages are extensively used. For easy understanding and assimilation of data, bar diagrams, pie diagram and simple graphs are also made use of in order to examine the relationship between two variables. Chi-Square tests are applied.

DEVELOPMENT OF QUESTIONNAIRE

- *Questionnaire – I:* The present study is based on the primary as well as secondary data. To collect the primary date two questionnaires are used one for SHGs and another one for banks. The questionnaires used for collecting the data from SHGs consist of twelve parts. Part one covers general information about the SHGs, second part covers the capital resources of the SHGs. Investment of the SHG in the form of bank deposits, internal lending, buildings and business is the third matter. Fourth, fifth and sixth part of the questionnaire consists savings, internal lending and the purpose for which loan is given by the SHGs respectively. The seventh and eighth part contains annual income of the SHG members and annual expenditure of the SHGs. Part nine relates to information relating to Bank operations such as deposits, borrowings, purpose-wise borrowings, rate of interest, ratio of loan on deposits, nature of security, subsidy etc. Utilisation and impact of bank loan is the subject matter covered in part ten and eleven of the questionnaire. The last part consists of questions relating to repayment of loan by the SHGs and members views on the benefits of joining the SHGs.
- *Questionnaire – II:* The questionnaire used for collecting the information from the banks consists of 8 parts. The first part contains general information such as name of the bank, location, name of the respondent, number of SHGs in the branch, saving amount, amount financed, number of beneficiaries and their savings year-wise, etc. Part two consists, determination of the loan amount and the purposes for which loan to the SHGs are given. Part three relates to number of loan accounts of SHGs, total year wise-loan amount, year-wise purpose wise-loan amount, interest on loan to SHGs, documents obtained, details of repeat loan and per cent of loan advanced to SHGs on their deposits etc. Section four and five contains questions relating to pre sanction measures and utilisation of the loan by the SHGs respectively. Sixth part of the questionnaire consists of recovery of loan from the SHGs. Seventh part contains training imparted to the SHG and the last part of the questionnaire is related to the impact of bank finances on the SHGs.

LOCALE OF THE STUDY

Belgaum revenue division also recognised as Mumbai Karnataka region is one of the four divisions of Karnataka state of India. After 1956, the new recognised State was divided into four divisions like Belgaum which had earlier been the headquarters of the southern division under the Bombay Presidency. It lies on the north-west of Karnataka State. The region consisting of seven districts namely: *(i)* Belgaum, *(ii)* Bagalkot, *(iii)* Bijapur, *(iv)* Dharwad, *(v)* Gadag, *(vi)* Haveri and *(vii)* Uttar Kannada. Totally it covers a geographical area of 54,538 sq. kms and has a population of 13,042,163 as of the 2001 census. The population density of the division is 239 per sq. kms. Hubli is the largest city in this region.

Belgaum District

Belgaum district is a district in the state of Karnataka. The city of Belgaum is the district head quarters. By 2011 census of India, it had a population of 47, 78,439 of which 24.3 per cent were urban making it a most populous district in Karnataka. The district has an area of 13415 sq. kms and is bounded on the west and north by Maharashtra State, on the north-east by Bijapur district, on the east by Bagalakot district, on the south-east by Gadag district, on the south by Dharwad district and Utter Kannada district, and on the south-west by the State of Goa. Administration of Belgaum district has been divided into 10 talukas such as: *(i)* Athani, *(ii)* Belgaum, *(iii)* Bailhongal, *(iv)* Chikkodi, *(v)* Gokak, *(vi)* Hukkeri, *(vii)* Khanapur, *(viii)* Raibag, *(xi)* Ramadurg and *(x)* Soundatti. Chikkodi taluka is the largest with an area of 1995.70 sq. kms and Raibag taluka is the smallest with an area of 958.80 sq. kms.

Belgaum is the commercial hub and stands second to Bangalore in terms of overall exports in the state. The district is important location for vegetables, fruits, meat, poultry, fish, wood, and mining production trading in north Karnataka, and is mainly traded with Goa. Rich deposits of bauxite are found in the district. Belgaum is the major producer of milk in Karnataka. It is a strong hub for machine shops catering to automotive manufacturing.

Bagalkot District

With reorganisation of the district in 1997, the new Bagalkot has come into existence during 50th year of India's independence.

The Bagalkot district bifurcated from Bijapur district and consists of six C. D. blocks namely: *(i)* Badami, *(ii)* Bagalkot, *(iii)* Bilagi, *(iv)* Hunugund, *(v)* Jamakhandi and *(vi)* Mudhol. The district is located in the north-western part of Karnataka. The most elevated portion of the district lies between 450 to 800 meters above the sea level extends over an area of 6593 sq. kms. The district is bounded by Bijapur district towards north, Gadag district towards south, Raichur district towards east, Koppal district towards south-east and Belgaum district towards south.

Agriculture is the largest employer in Bagalkot with over 65 per cent of the working population engaged in it. Approximately 80 per cent of male workers are engaged in agriculture. Bagalkot district is rich in black soil which is conducive to the growth of cotton. The approximate per capita income is US $ 360. The chief crops cultivated are jowar, wheat, as well as groundnut, cotton, maze bajra, sugarcane and tobacco. Famine due to lack of adequate rains is quite common in Bagalkot district. The sizeable proportion of the population also consists of weavers. The chief manufacturing products are cotton and silk cloths. Large quantities of cotton yarn are also dyed and exported to other of the states and the country.

Bijapur District

Bijapur district is in the north-western part of Karnataka, bounded by Maharashtra State and Gulbarga district in the north, Bagalkot district in the south, Gulbarga and Raichur district in the east and Belgaum district in the west. The district lies between north latitude 15.20° to 17.20° and East longitude 74.50° to 76.29°. The district has five talukas namely: *(i)* Basavana-Bagewadi, *(ii)* Bijapur, *(iii)* Indi, *(iv)* Muddebihal and *(v)* Sindgi. The Bijapur taluka is the biggest one whereas the Muddebihal taluka is the smallest taluka in terms of geographical area. As per 2011 census the population of the district was 2,175,102 with a literacy rate of 67.20 per cent. The male literacy rate was 77.41 per cent and Female literacy rate was 56.54 per cent. Agriculture is the main occupation of the people in the district and it largely depends on natural rain. The district receives small amount of rainfall every year and many times it was declared by the Government of Karnataka as draught prone area. The temperature varies from 16°C to 44°C. summer is very hot and winter and rainy seasons are cool. Since the area is receiving small amount of rainfall, the district possesses considerably less forest area. It has 1977 hectares of forest area which is about 0.18 per cent of the total geographical area. Jowar, bajra, wheat, maize, sugarcane, oil seeds and cotton are the main agricultural crops and gram, tur are the main pulses. Besides these, lemon, grapes, pomegranate, banana, mango are the horticultural products and tomato, brinjol, onion and chilly are the major vegetable crops grown in the district.

Dharwad District

Dharwad district is situated in the western sector of the northern half of Karnataka State. The district encompasses an area of 4263 sq. kms lying between a latitudinal parallels of 15.02 degree and 15.51 degree north and longitudes of 73.43 degree and 75.35 degree east. The district is bounded on the north by the district of Belgaum, on the east by the district of Gadag, on the south by Haveri and on the west by Uttar Kannada district. All these districts belong to Karnataka State itself. According to 2011 census, the district has a population of 1,846,993. This gives it a ranking of 256th in India. The district has a population density of 434 inhabitants per sq. kms. The literacy rate is 80.3 per cent.

This region on an average receives moderate to heavy rainfall and have dense vegetation. Kalghatagi and Alnavar area in Dharwad taluka in particular receive more rainfall than other talukas of the district. On the agriculture front, the presence of black soil helps in raising crops like cotton, wheat, ragi, jowar and oil seeds and that of red soil is more suitable for paddy.

The district falls in tropical region which is largely affected by monsoons'. This explains that the district is an agro-based economy, and also that agriculture is the main occupation in whole of rural area of the district. The other activities of economy that is trade and commerce are completely dependent on agriculture. As monsoons are highly uncertain in nature and as there is no major irrigation project or any hydel power generating station in the district. There is high degree of high land farming. The mineral wealth is not quite impressive and forest wealth is equally unattractive. Manufacturing industry, particularly agro-based industry makes a significant contribution to the economy. Of the total population 39 per cent makes up for working class. This consists of 26 per cent of those engaged in agricultural sector. Till today agriculture is a labour intensive enterprise. Many labourers largely depend on seasonal employment. The per capita income at current prices is Rs. 14861. The State level per capita income at current prices is Rs. 14909. The main kharif crops are cotton, chilies, sugarcane and groundnuts and the main Rabi crops are jowar, wheat, rice, etc.

The human development index is .64 where as that of Karnataka .65. In the three backward talukas of Dharwad district, the state Government adult literacy scheme that is community learning and vocational training was in force.

Gadag District

The district is situated on the north east of the erstwhile Dharwad district. The district is bounded on the north by Bagalkot district, on the east by Koppal district, on the southeast by Bellary district, on the southwest by Haveri district, on west by Dharwad district and on the northwest by Belgaum district. The district lies between 14.52 north latitudinal parallels and 75.17 and 76.02 east longitudinal parallels. The district has five talukas namely: *(i)* Gadag-Betageri, *(ii)* Mundargi, *(iii)* Naragund, *(iv)* Ron and *(v)* Shirahatti. According to 2011 senses, Gadag district has a population of 1,065,235. This gives it a ranking of 426 in India. The district has a population density of 229 inhabitants per sq. kms. The literacy rate of the district is 75.18 per cent.

The absence of any irrigation project in the district highlights the vulnerability of the agricultural economy and emphasises the importance of dry land farming in its overall economy. The right bank canal of Malaprabha Project irrigates the entire Naragund taluka and portion of Ron taluka (12 villages). The other sources are tanks, wells, and lift irrigation.

Gadag is a major industrial centre. Due to slow improvement in infrastructure, especially power and transport, industrial growth has been slow. The small scale industries in the district constituted about 1.9 per cent of the total units in Karnataka. The district accounted for 2.9 per cent of small scale sector employment in the state. About 25 per cent of the workers are self-employed in the district.

Haveri District

Haveri is the district in the state of Karnataka. The district was earlier part of undivided Dharwad district. Haveri district is popularly known for Byadagi chilli variety and its market in South East Asia. The district situated between 14.28 to 14.39 north latitudinal parallels and 75.07 to 75.38 east longitudinal parallels. It is surrounded by Dharwad district on the north, Gadag district on the northeast, Bellary on the east Davanagere on the south, Shimoga district on southeast and Uttar Kannada district on the west and northwest respectively. According to 2011 census, Haveri district has a population of 1,598,506. This gives it a ranking 312 in India. The district has a population density of 331 per sq. kms and has a literacy rate of 77.6 per cent.

79 per cent of the total population lives in rural areas. The S. C. population is 12.18 per cent and S. T. population is 08.48 per cent of the total population while OBC and general is 78.98 per cent of the total population. The agricultural workers are 11.19 per cent (male) and 02.96 per cent (female), while the non-agricultural workers are over 43.49 per cent (male) and 27.75 per cent (female). Cereals mainly jowar, maize, paddy and ragi are grown in the district. The important cash crops grown in the district are groundnut, pulses, chilies and cotton. Mango, sapota, banana, lime are the horticultural crops grown in the district.

Uttar Kannada District

Uttar Kannada is also known as North Canara or North Kanara. It is one of the biggest districts of Karnataka State with abundant natural resources. The district has a variety of geographical features with thick forest, perennial rivers and abundant flora and fauna and a long coastal line of about 140 kms. in length.

The district is surrounded by Belgaum and the State of Goa in the north, by Dharwad district in the east, by Shimoga district and Udupi district in the south, Arabian Sea from the west borders. The administration of the district has been divided into 11 talukas. They are: *(i)* Ankola, *(ii)* Bhatkal, *(iii)* Haliyal, *(iv)* Honnavar, *(v)* Joida, *(vi)* Kumuta, *(vii)* Karwar, *(viii)* Mundgoad, *(ix)* Sirsi, *(x)* Siddapur and *(xi)* Yallapur. According to 2011 census Uttar Kannada district has a population of 1,436,847. This gives it a ranking of 346 in India. The district has a population density of 140 inhabitants per sq. kms. The literacy rate is 84.03 per cent.

The main geographic feature of the district is the Western Ghats or Sahyadri range which runs from north to south through the district. The district high rainfall supports lush forests which covers approximately 70 per cent of the district. In its 10.25 lakh hectares of total land, of which 8.28 hectares is forest land. Only about 1.2 lakh hectares of land is under agriculture-horticulture.

Though the district is located in coastal area, it is not so famous for its marine products. But, activities connected with fisheries are carried out on large scales with the help of State Government as well as Central Government. The major population lives in rural areas under taking agriculture as their main occupation. The main traditional occupations are agriculture, fisheries, animal Husbandry, sericulture, horticulture, beekeeping and leather works etc. The main tribes of the district are Sidhi, Kunabi, Halakki, Vokkaliga, Gonda and Gouli.

SCOPE OF THE STUDY

The present study covers seven districts and forty nine talukas of Belgaum division of Karnataka state. The study is confined to SHG based micro-financing; particularly SHG-bank Linkage programme however, it has its implications on the empowerment of the poor.

LIMITATIONS OF THE STUDY

The limitations of the study are as follows:

- Data collection from the banks posed a major problem as the banks are reluctant to divulge certain information.
- Poverty and poor education level of the respondents posed difficulties in getting accurate information.
- Getting the actual figures for the groups is very difficult because of their unsystematic way of record keeping.
- Though the investigator had taken at most care while collecting data possibility of some errors creeping in cannot be ruled out.
- The study relied heavily on respondents' memory to gather information pertaining to certain variables.
- The information provided by the banks is approximate figures.

RESEARCH DESIGN

The Study has been arranged in six chapters:

Chapter – I: Introduction

The introduction chapter projects the significance of micro-finance in the economic development of India. Besides, the chapter deals with the concept of micro-finance, micro-credit–historical perspective, socio-economic impact of micro-finance, current Indian socio-economic scenario, origin of the research problem, significance of the study, objectives, methodology, development of the questionnaire, locale of the study, limitations of the study, study area and research design.

Chapter – II: Review of Literature

The second chapter highlights the review of earlier literature concerning the topic of research.

Chapter – III: SHG-Bank-Linkage Programme

The third chapter deals with SHG-Bank Linkage Programme in India, in Karnataka and in the study area.

Chapter – IV: Economic Impact of Micro-finance through SHGs

The fourth chapter analyses the economic impact of micro-financing through SHGs in the study area.

Chapter – V: Social Impact of Micro-finance through SHGs

The fifth chapter deals with the social impact of micro-financing through SHGs in the study area.

Chapter – VI: Findings and Suggestions

The findings and suggestions are presented the sixth chapter.

2

REVIEW OF EARLIER LITERATURE

The review of literature plays a crucial role in establishing back-drop for any research work. It is a fact that justification of the present study can be clarified by reviewing the available literature on the subject to find out the gap of the research study.

Singh (1995) conceptualized SHG as an informal association of individuals which come together voluntarily for the promotion of economic and social objectives.

Prasad (1995) conducted a study on 'Development of Women and Children in Rural Areas – Successful Case Studies'. DWCRA is being implemented in 354 districts all over the country as a sub-scheme of IRDP. The objective of the programme is to raise the income level of women of poor household and enable them to become organized participants in social development and economic self-reliance. Besides providing financial support for income-generating activities, it also aims at increasing women's access to other welfare service. With this objective the present study was undertaken in Gurgaon district of Haryana. Some of the common factors for the success of the group are homogeneity, effective leadership; repayment procedures, systematic planning, quality control and marketing, support of officials are the key factors for the effective management of the programme.

Choudhary (1996) in her study stressed the need for shaping women's empowering strategies to make them effective and result oriented. She pointed out that money earned by poor women is more likely to be spent on the basic needs of life than that by men and that this realisation would bring women as the focus of development efforts. She also examined the advantage of organizing women groups there by creating a new sense of dignity and confidence to tackle their problems with a sense of solidarity and to work together for the cause of economic independence.

Yadagiri (1996) conducted a study on 'Rural Poor and a Challenging Task of DWCRA: A Study of Women in A. P'. The area selected was Nedunoor Village in Rangareddy district. DWCRA programme seeks to provide opportunities of Self-employment on a sustained basis. The women have also become socially aware of the need to educate the girl child and prevent social evils such as liquor consumption and child marriage. One women group organizer said that we have now realised that both boys and girls are the same, our daughters could also become collectors if they are educated. DWCRA members said it resulted in better quality of life because of access to literacy and health services. There is also betterment in nutritional status of families.

Karmakar (1998) defined SHG as an informal group of people where members pool their savings and relend within the group on rotational basis.

Shylendra (1998) defined SHGs are small informal associations created for the purpose of enabling members to reap economic benefit out of mutual help, solidarity and joint responsibility. The group-based approach not only enables the poor to accumulate capital by way of small savings but also helps them to get access to formal credit facilities.

Medha (2001) made a study similar to that of Sebastian, but Medha also covered the SHGs promoted by government agencies also in Maharashtra state. The title of the study was 'Mobilizing Women SHGs through Government and Non-Government Organizations'. Which attempted to focus that how various governmental and empower women through Self-help groups (SHGs). Total 160 SHGs selected from three taluks *viz.*, Bhor, Velha and Havele of Maharashtra.

Titus and Sebastian (2001) made a study on impact of micro-credit programme operated by NGOs on rural women and the title of the study was 'Impact of Micro-credit Programme of NGOs on Rural Women'.

Basu *et al.* (2002) made a similar study on empowerment of women and the title of the study was 'Empowerment of Women in the Context of Development Some Issues and Suggestions'.

Gupta (2002) made a study on 'Formation and Functioning of SHGs in Hoshangabad District of Madhya Pradesh' with the objective to examine the working of, Self-Help Groups in the state of Madhya Pradesh, in general, and in village Dande jundar, in particular. Dandi Jundar in Kesla block of Hoshangabad district was selected for the study. The village is having eight SHGs and the district has the largest number of SHGs in the state. Data were collected from the branches of the State bank of India, District Co-operative bank, Regional Rural Bank at Suktawa and Co-operative society in the same village, which catered to the needs of SHGs of the village. Discussions were also held with the members of SHGs to get the information.

Jyothy (2002) made a study on SHGs in Tamil Nadu titled 'Self-Help Groups under the Women's Development Programmes in Tamil Nadu: Achievements, Bottlenecks and Recommendations' and found that women development depends upon capacity building, awareness and health, education, environment, legal rights, functional literacy and numeracy, communication skills, leadership skills for self and mutual help. Economic empowerment of women is also vital and the study profiles self-help groups of Mahalir Thittam (Women's Development Programme) in Tamil Nadu and there are over 26,000 groups as on March 2000 in the state. The data on self-help groups reveal high degree of motivation and determination to succeed. On the basis of indicators, the growth of self-help groups and its members, percentage of SC and ST members, growth of savings and internal lending are discussed. The economic activities of SHG groups include production and marketing of agarbathis, candles and soaps, readymade garments, pickles, papads and other items. The self-help groups are also enable women to perform various self-sustained activities, such as proper functioning of the ration shops, maintain vigil to prevent brewing of illicit-liquor, help the aged, deserted and widows, grow vegetables in their kitchen gardens and maintaining group unity and transcend barriers of caste, creed and religion. External credit linkage is essential to foster the financial sustainability of the SHGs. The study recommends removal of bias against SHGs by the bank officials, and each bank should have a special cell to assess the activities of SHGs and clusters should also be favorably disposed towards them to sustain the programme.

Reddy (2002) in his study on 'Empowering Women through Self-Help Groups and Micro-Credit: The Case of NIRD Action Research Projects' made an attempt on how Self-Help Groups promoted among women as part of Action Research leads to women empowerment. The study describes that thrift and credit was strategic entry point for the action research intervention in Ranga Reddy district of Andhra Pradesh.

Patil (2002) conducted a study on 'Rural Development Programmes and their Impact on Women Beneficiaries of Dharwad District of Karnataka during 1999-2000'. Selection of villages was done by random sampling technique and 120-beneficiaries from eight villages were selected purposively who had taken self-employment as a venture. The information about various developmental programmes being implemented in the Dharwad district was collected from the Block Development Office and Zilla Perished. Out of those different schemes TRYSEM and DWCRA programmes were selected, because these programmes helped maximum number of women beneficiaries to start self-employment. The independent variables selected for the study were, age, education, occupation, caste, marital status, type of family, family sizes, type of house, land holding, annual family income, social participation and mass media participation. Knowledge was collected by personal interview method by using pre-tested schedule.

Sarada Devi and Rayalu (2002) in their study on 'Factors Functioning in Women Empowerment in Urban Areas Conducted in Hyderabad', identify various aspects related to the empowerment of women and assess the level of differences between working and non-working women in the perception of women's empowerment. Seventy-five working and 75 non-working women were selected randomly from the twin cities of Hyderabad and Secunderabad of Andhra Pradesh. Data were collected though interview schedules. Study showed that working women perceived more problems due to more power in the family than non-working Women. Non-working women faced problems due to powerlessness when compared to working women. Non-women women had more aspirations related to power as they were deprived of required power status in the family. Both working and non-working women felt that their personal freedom and self-interest were their first priority in power persuasion. The power ratio was better for the working women than non-working women and more number of non-working women used different strategies to get power. More number of non-working women perceived discomfort in performing their daily roles and experienced more restrictions on them as compared to the working women. Lacks of freedom to spend money, inability to pursue self-interests, loss of personal affairs were the problems experienced by the non-working women.

Amin (2003) evaluate whether micro-credit programmes such as the popular Grameen Bank reach the relatively poor and vulnerable in two Bangladesh villages. By using a unique panel dataset with monthly consumption and income data for 229 households they found that while micro-credit is successful at reaching the poor, it is less successful at reaching the vulnerable. Their results also suggest that micro-credit is unsuccessful at reaching the group most prone to destitution, the vulnerable poor.

Dr. N. Lalitha (2003) in her book 'Mainstreaming Micro-finance', reviews the progress of financing in India, analyses the benefit share of women in the total credit off take under conventional lending, examines the credit delivery system, credit utilisation and benefit outflow under micro-finance programme and suggests measures for the effective operations of micro-finance.

Dr. N. Lalitha (2003) in her 'Mainstreaming Micro-finance' reviews the progress of micro-finance operations in India, analysis the benefit share of women in the total credit off-take in the study area under conventional lending, examines the credit delivery system, credit utilisation and benefit out flow under micro-finance programme and suggests measures for the effective operations of micro-finance on the basis of the outcome of the study. The book presents a vivid and penetrating analysis of the micro-finance activities at macro as well as micro-level.

In the past Puyalvannan (2003) made a study on SHGs in Tamil Nadu. The study Micro-credit innovations: a study based on 'Micro-credit, Women empowerment and living of SHGs with co-operative banks in two districts in Tamil Nadu', was conducted in Trichy and Pudukkottai district of Tamil Nadu. The study revealed that, SHGs has formed by fifteen approved NGOs in the Pudukkottai and Trichy districts. The members have granted loans for varieties of purposes, both productive and unproductive. Results have shown that women are credit worthy and responsible users of credit. Recovery is monitored by the group members and they are discussed regularly in the group and group meetings. The recovery is reported to be 90 per cent in the Pudukkottai district. Social impacts of SHGs operation in the areas show that the women members have achieved political empowerment by winning elections in panchayat boards. SHGs have established effective networking with other government organizations, NGOs etc. Many SHGs were given micro-entrepreneurship training and they have equipped the members to do varieties of activities.

Saharan (2003) conducted a study on SHGs and empowerment found that the participation in the self-help groups enriched the women in house managements, health and sanitation, leadership qualities and economically. The decision-making capacity of the SHG participants increased with the period of participation.

V. M. Rao (2004) in his book entitled 'Empowering Rural Women' makes an attempt to understand the nature and impact of STEP programmed on women and to draw lessons for future policy exercises.

Mohammad Yunus (2004) in his article 'Grameen Bank, Micro-credit and Millennium Development Goals' traces the evolution of the ideas and practice of micro-credit as pioneered by the Grameen Bank. Over the years, micro-credit programme in Bangladesh have grown, providing a wide range of services to meet the economic and social needs of citizens, mostly poor women. It comes up with suggestions regarding the emerging issues of financial self-reliance and institutional sustainability of micro-credit programmes.

Rao and Sarojanis (2005) conducted a study on 'Tribal Self-Help Groups – Strengths and Weaknesses' and revealed that majority of the sample have inclination and interest towards political participation and are well aware about banking system.

M. Ramanjaneyalu (2006) in his book entitled 'Economic Empowerment of Women in India', made an enquiry in the favorable circumstance for women to ventures, motivational factors, socio-economic and managerial aspects of tangible and intangible benefits of the women micro-enterprises in Karnataka state in India. The study also represents physical and financial achievements of various institutions that extended support credit for woman development in the state.

Hiatt and Woodworth (2006) in their study on Central America found that micro-finance clients' socio-economic and economic levels had increased due to their continued participation. Micro-credit appears to improve the lives of those who are poor by increasing their buying and investing capability, thus lifting them onto a higher economic plane. Accordingly, these small loans seem to positively affect poverty by creating entrepreneurship and greater self-reliance among the poor.

Thomas Dichter and Malcolm Harper (2007) in their book entitled 'What's with Micro-finance', aimed to sound a timely warning to government, bankers donors and the general public. The intention is not to halt or slow micro-finance initiatives but to encourage a reassessment of experiences and a rethink of expectations and policies. Micro-finance can never be a panacea and May sometimes is an activity damaging to its intended customers. It is a timely collection of export treatises questioning the scope and rationales for micro-finance. Specifically aimed at giving a reality check at a time when hype around micro-finance potential has never been greater.

Prabhu Ghate (2007) in his book entitled 'Indian Micro-finance – The Challenges of Rapid Growth' has made an attempt to put together a one step document that will help a variety of readers catch-up on the latest developments issues and achievements of the micro-finance sector in India. The sector is growing rapidly both in the scale and in the diversity of actors and is sitting on the cusp of regulation. It is therefore in the midst of rapid flux. The book is in a sense a snapshot of the sector.

I. Satya Sundaram (2007) in his book entitled 'Micro-finance in India' has made an attempt as to how micro-finance in India has led to the real empowerment of the rural poor, particularly women. He has made a reference of the problem of the banking sector and the innovative scheme introduced by the banks to help the poor. He made in his book, stress on educating the member on social issues.

Aloysius, P. Fernandez and Vidya Ramachandran (2007) have made a study on 'Self-Help Group approach in Karnataka'. The study revealed that, self-help group approach in Karnataka has been developed on the basis of 'only that much is true of the other person as is true of me' understanding. There is respect for people, belief in their basic ability to take responsible decisions, awareness that affinity based peer relationships can transform individual energies into collective strengths and recognition that a system that works requires a structured institutional framework that not only offers spaces and opportunities for development but also anchors it in a stable system of operating norms.

Monika Tushar, Sumita Chadda and Pankaj Ahlawat (2007) in their study on 'Role of Micro-finance to Uplift the Economic Conditions of Women Households in Haryana through SHGs' revealed that the SHG bank-linkage programme had offered greater opportunities for closer interaction between banks and group members. There is a significant improvement in the recent years and the concept has picked up with the constant support of the state government banks and NGOs. The SHG has helped the poor mosses in earning their living, generating staff employment and maintaining their living standard.

K. Prabakhar Rajkumar (2007) in his study on 'Empowerment of Rural Women through NABARD and Promotional Activities' found that, empowering women is a sure way to link growth and human development. NABARD's financial assistance, through various schemes makes the rural women equal partners in the economic prosperity of India.

Anil K. Khandelwal (2007) made a study on 'Micro-finance Development Strategy for India' and found that, micro-finance is still an evolving sector in a country like India, in many developed countries it is highly commercialized; partnership are being created, public and private sector assets are being leveraged, and know-how is being shared. The lessons from some of the best managed micro-finance institutions around the world show that, the use of certain methods like group lending, peer guarantees, step ladder lending, matching repayment terms with borrower cash-flow etc., have contributed largely to their success. Also, they have completely used information technologies and performance linked incentives for their staff.

The micro-finance portfolio would enable commercial banks to diversify their operations considerably. However, the co-ordinate and collaborative approach alone would be the right answer to bring marginalized communities into the main stream of the national economy. The continuous flow of innovations in designing new product and services would produce the desired result on a sustainable basis.

P. Satish (2007) made a study on the criticism of the draft micro-finance bill, reveals an ignorance of facts and offers groundless criticism of the public sector institutions involved.

M. S. Sriram, Radhakumar (2007) in their study 'Conditions in Which Micro-financed has Emerged in Certain Regions' focused on the availability of infrastructure, economic growth, density of population and the availability of formal financial services to examine if any of these factors explain its growth of micro-finance in certain regions.

Jairam Ramesh (2007) in his article focused an Andhra model. SHGs, the major form of delivery of micro-finance in India, have brought about dramatic changes in the lives of lakhs of women. In Andhra Pradesh, which has the largest network of SHGs and where the Government has been a strong supporter; they have gone beyond provision of credit and assured many non-traditional responsibilities. The Andhra model is one that other state should consider replicating.

Sunita Premchandra and M. Chidamberanatham (2007) focused their study on proposed amendments to NABARD Act 1981, finds that, the proposed amendments to the NABARD Act that seeks to provide a formal framework for the micro-finance sector does not take a gender or empowerment perspective, but rather, a supply dominated view of micro-finance.

H. Shylendra (2007) in his study on micro-finance bill and found that, the micro-finance sector (development and regulation) bill-2007, which has attracted criticism on many counts, aims to ensure that, NGOs use their social mediation skills to ensure financial intermediation. However, the bills ambit is narrow and it fails to take major aspects of micro-finance delivery into account.

Jasprect Kaur Soni (2008) in his book entitled 'Women Empowerment – The Substantial Challenges' has made an effort to bring to the public a comprehensive view of the current scenario of women's participation. The main creative competencies of women relate to innovation, judgment opportunity recognition, relationship building and protectiveness, which give women a distinct competitive advantage. Creative opportunities are derived from awareness, access to education and social networks and previous and recent problems. Women empowerment is verily at the centre of great attention among economists, sociologists, politicians and of course national and state strategies. This book is an attempt to present all the development of women empowerment in a simplistic yet utilitarian perspective.

S. K. Das, B. P. Nanda and J. Rath (2008) Edited the book entitled 'Micro-finance and Rural Development in India', contains the research articles relating to various topics of micro-finance ranging from micro-finance, SHG, bank-linkage programme etc.

Awadhesh Kumar Singh (2008) in his book 'Empowering Rural Women through Micro Financing' reviewed the functioning and performance of Swashakti and Swoyamsiddha project in India and suggested policy measures for their effective functioning and improving performance.

A. P. Pati (2008) has made an attempt to study 'The Financial Sustainability of the SHGs Engaged in the Business of Micro-credit in the State of Meghalaya'. As observed from the secondary sources the grading of groups and recovery of the SHG financing in Meghalaya is precarious. Many have formed groups because of subsidy provision in the SGSY scheme and this has made the scheme very popular in the state. The primary survey on 200 SHGs, though reveals a sustainable financial operation of simple groups during the study period, sustainability becomes less attractive when the subsidy is negotiated in the financial details. The study shows that, there is a negative impact of subsidy on financial sustainability of SHG operations, which should be curbed by encouraging group formations with non-subsidized finance.

M. A. Lokhande (2008) has undertaken a study to find out whether SHGs are really helpful in eradicating poverty of poor members? Are SHGs instrumental in enhancing economic and social status of the members? To what extent, SHGs are mobilizing funds and generating income in Marathwada Region. The study observed that, the slow progress of SHG bank linkage programme in Marathwada was due to shortage of capable promotional institutions, hesitation on the part of the banks as loans to SHGs are collateral free, dependency of SHGs on promoting agencies for routine work such as convening and conducting meeting, maintaining books of accounts etc., lack of entrepreneurial training and skill up gradation facilities, imbalanced growth of SHGs.

M. S. Gupta (2008) in his study stressed the need of Governments participation in promoting the SHGs. He also pointed out that, there is a need to stress on extensive awareness campaign, skill development and training programme, co-ordination between banks and SHGs, effective flow of credit for a strong follow up in these states where it is at nascent stage. In order to solve the problems relating to marketing of SHGs, the state level organizations and NGOs should come forward and extend facilities especially in empowering women entrepreneurs by providing education, motivation, training, and financial help and so on. It is also important to develop a proper regulatory structure for micro-finance institutions for healthy growth of the sector along with supportive refinance, legal framework and capacity building measures.

Goutam Kanwar, R. Kartikeya, Rajat Kapoor and Rajat K. Bisoyi (2008) in their study 'Micro-finance in the Indian Scenario: A Study on the Existing Models' made an attempt give a comprehensive overview of all aspects of micro-finance in India – its essence, the different institutions involved in its promotion, the different modes of delivery, its weakness and the challenges that lie ahead.

I. Narendra Kumar and A. C. Komala (2008) in their study, examined the group lending mechanism used by the SHG linked programmes and examined how implementing of full and immediate joint liability and restricting the number of simultaneous borrowers in a group enhances the SHGs. Along with giving the poor access to credit the mechanism also allows the poor obtain a premium on their savings.

M. Karunakar and S. Saravanan (2008) made a study on 'Impact of Micro-finance on SHGs in Tamil Nadu', found that, in the most part of the country SHGs have achieved success in bringing the women in mainstream of decision-making. SHGs are also viable organized set up to disburse micro-credit to the needy entrepreneur women and encouraging their promotion of poverty alleviation activities and programmes.

Abraham Punnoose (2008) in his study on 'Micro-finance Scenario of Kerala' and revealed that, the obsession of micro-finance towards setting up of micro-enterprise is still elusive in Kerala in view of the specific realities of the state. Micro-finance can not replace the inherent allied inputs like input market support, appropriate skill and technology, working capital etc. It is considered as livelihood finance to meet the distressing environment of the state of Kerala.

Sayantan Bera (2008) in his study made an attempt to conflate the activities of the SHGs and their federations, the Grameen Bank replicators and commercial micro-finance institutions, leading to the belief that in empowering the poor the positive attributes of one are shared by the other.

Rajaram Dasgupta (2008) in his study viewed that India's draft legislation on micro-finance suffers in comparison with the law in Bangladesh. The main demand for the legislation in India has arisen from the need to create a new set of financial institutions providing micro-finance services but the MFDRD proposes to give a certificate to few types of existing institutions and does not consider NBFCs and Section 250 companies for its certificates.

Debanarayan Sarkar (2008) made a study on 'Indian Micro-finance: Lessons from Bangladesh' traces the fundamental differences in the provision of micro-credit between Indian mainstream banks and the Bangladesh Grameen bank.

S. Mahendra Dev and C. Ravi (2008) in their study on 'Revising Estimates of Poverty' estimates poverty ratio at the all India level and for the states in 2004-05 by including the minimum private expenditure on health and education. The estimated poverty ratios are substantially higher than the official ratio.

Martin Ravallion (2008) discussed in his study the methodology underlying the World Bank's recent revised estimates of global poverty and then analyses the Indian numbers.

Frances Sinha (2009) in his book entitled micro-finance Self-Help Groups in India living up to their promise, focused on the promotion and operation of SHGs, how member related to one another, how groups interacted with their communities, as well as the effect groups had on their social, political and economic environments and vice versa. The study as thorough divided into many questions with a verity of techniques, and took great pains to respect the privacy of villagers as they confided their experiences. The result is a rich profile both quantitative and qualitative of rural self-help in India.

Jayasheela, Shri Prasad H. and Dinesha P. T. (2009) in their book tried to explain the meaning and working of micro-finance and SHGs and explain how micro-finance leads to women empowerment.

Dr. N. Jayaselan (2009) in the book entitled 'Micro-credit to Micro-enterprise – Opportunities and Challenges for Self-Help Groups' primarily attempts to find out how the continuous access to SHG based micro-finance programme has promoted the micro-finance enterprises its impact on the management of micro-enterprises and also to identity the factors that promote thwart the promotion of the micro-enterprises. It also looked in to the changes in the entrepreneurial behavioural competencies of SHG women and evaluates the changes in terns of employment level, income and assets of the SHG women pre- SHG and post SHG period. The book has suggested measures for policy changes for better implementation of SHG bank-linkage and micro-enterprise development programme.

Kank Kanti Bagchi (2009) in his book 'Micro-finance and Rural Development' Critically deals with the role of micro-finance in rural development in India It Contains 23 papers and most of the papers are empirical in nature in that the papers involve field study and therefore reveal the experiences of the scholars regarding the role of micro-credit in rural development. The common tenor of all the paper is that micro-finance has helped the empowerment of rural folk who are members of SHGs a number of ways though it is not a panacea for rural development and empowerment of rural population due to multipurpose problem associated with beneficiaries and the lending institutions and the intermediaries.

A. Vijaykumar (2009) in his book entitled 'Banking Micro-finance and SHGs in India' contains 25 research papers focusing on varied aspects of Indian banking, Micro-finance and SHGs, Penned with an in depth analysis by academic and research scholars. The book will be of immense help in the study of new innovations in Indian banking in the changing global business scenario.

Dr. Devendra Prasad Pandey (2009) in his book 'Micro-Finance Management' contains the detailed information on the management aspects of micro-finance institutions.

Dr. Rais Ahmed (2009) in the book series 1, 2, 3 entitled 'Micro-finance and Women Empowerment' has been divided in to three parts, incorporates articles/research paper contributed by scholars. The contributors have presented their views analytically which are connected with the different aspects of micro-finance and SHGs performance and their role in socio-economic empowerment of women. The papers contributed for this book have been grouped into different sections.

Mandakini Das and Pritirekha Daspattanayak (2009) in the book 'Empowering Women Issues Challenges and Strategies' is a unique compilation of selected research based papers focusing attention on the empowerment process of women both from a global perspective as well as from the Indian angle of vision. It covers the whole gamut of problems and prospects of the ensuring empowerment process.

Chakradhar Satapathy, Sabita Mishra and Kalyan Ghadei (2009) in their book entitled 'Empowerment of Women – Perception and Realities' examines the socio-cultural background, government policy role of development agencies and capacity building of individuals in deciding the women related programmes. Efforts have been made to define and operationally different concepts on women issue based research and experience.

D. Sundar Ram (2009) in his book 'Women Empowerment in Political Institutions – An Indian Perspective' is a collection of fourteen original essays by prominent policy makers, academicians, researchers, social workers and women activists at the National conference. This book brings together a range of perspectives concerning the causes and solution to the problem of women political empowerment in India.

Christabell P.J. (2009) in her book entitled 'Women Empowerment through Capacity Building? The Role of Micro-finance', assesses the role of Micro-finance in building up economic and democratic capacity of women and thereby enhancing their empowerment in India, with special reference to the state of Kerala. Evaluating the performance of SHGs, it tries to identify the factors that contribute to their successful performance and sustainability. It also studies the level of participation of women in SHGs and examines the group dynamics that influence their participation.

P. B. Rathod (2009) in his book entitled 'Women and Development' contains women and development status and position of women in India, role of media in women development, socio-economic status of women, policy and planning, women employment crime against women etc.

Sangeeta Bharadwaj Badal (2009) in her book 'Gender, Social Structure and Empowerment – Status Report of Women in India', is the persistence of female male gaps in human development in India indicative of low status assigned to women in that cultural settings. It is observed that women's status is affected by kinship structures development level and social stratification, which very over space and time individually and in interaction with each other. It is this variation that leads to differences in women's position from one region of Indian to another.

S. K. Baral and S.C. Bihari (2010) in their book 'Rural Marketing and Micro-finance' dealt the opportunities for the FMCG producers to enter in to the rural market. They viewed that; there is a vast difference between the life styles of rural and urban consumers. The rural Indian consumer is economically, socially and psycho graphically different from urban counterpart hence the FMCG producers will have to consider all these things to enter in to the rural market.

T. Lavanya (2010) in her book entitled 'Women Empowerment through Entrepreneurship Focused on the Various Aspects of Women Entrepreneurship in India'. The book also explains the experience of other countries in this regard. It examines in detail the activities and problems of women entrepreneurs in an important state of India *viz;* A. P.

Ambika Prasad Pati (2010) in the book entitled 'Financial Sustainability of Micro-finance' precisely delves in to the aspect of sustainability of self-help groups and of the most acclaimed programme of micro-financing *i.e.* SHG bank-linkage (SBLP) programme lunched by NABARD in early nineties.

Neeta Tapan (2010) in her book 'Micro-credit Self-Help Groups (SHGs) and Women Empowerment', deals with the role of micro-credit and SHGs in the socio-economic empowerment of women. Micro-credit has emerged as the most suitable and practical alternatives to the conventional banking in reaching the hitherto unreached poor population. Micro-credit enables the poor people to the thrifty and helps them in availing the credit and other financial services for improving the living standards. The SBLP envisages organization of the rural poor in to SHGs for building their capacities to manage their own finance and then negotiate bank credit on commercial terms.

Dr. Tanuj Kumar Bisoyi (2010) in her book entitled 'Rural Credit, Regional Rural Banks and Micro-finance', contained important research write ups contributed by eminent researchers and professionals relating to the role of RRBs for economic development of women, especially in ameliorating the socio-economic backwardness.

Deepali Pant Joshi (2010) in her book 'Micro-finance for Macro Change Emerging Challenges' combines the detailed painstaking research of a noted scholar with the practical experience of the policy maker. It furnishes on extensive analysis of the remarkable traits that have ensured the success of micro-finance. The comprehensive overview takes due cognizance of emerging concerns and the new challenges confronting micro-finance in its bid to upscale beyond consumption lending. It sheds light on a host of contentious issues in micro-finance.

Surendra K. Koushik and V. Rengarajan (2010) in their book entitled 'Micro-finance and Women's Empowerment', highlighted the implementation of the government programmes exclusively for women. They have identified the shortcomings right from the stage of identification of the beneficiaries to the selection of the activities and their feasibility to the level of implementing agency, to the financing institution.

Krishna Gupta (2010) in his book entitled 'Empowerment of Women Emerging Dimensions' This book is the result of an interdisciplinary discourse attempting to unfold the various dimensions of women empowerment. Collection of paper in this volume highlights the fact that, women are more vulnerable than men because they represent the majority of word's poor section and suffer from multiple disabilities due to unequal wages legal constraints, lesser access to education, health and employment. The book has examined the emerging dimensions of empowerment in political economic and social spheres and calls for structural changes and social transformation to end gender inequalities.

Dr. R. N. Mishra and G. Chandrayya (2010) Edited the book entitled 'Micro-finance for Agricultural Development' contains 13 scholarly articles on various aspect of micro-finance and agricultural development. The book highlights the supply of credit and its proper use will increase the production and productivity of the agricultural sector. If loan is not used in a proper way it will not generate the repaying capacity of the borrowers an d it restrict the repayment of loan and create a burden for institutional agencies and government.

Pitta Usha (2010) in her book entitled 'Empowerment of Women and SHGs' is a comprehensive study on empowerment of women through SHGs. The study focuses on the working of SHGs of group level and also analyses the efficacy of SHG approach to micro-credit in empowering the poor women.

Sumalata (2010) in her book entitled 'Towards Empowering Women – Views and Reviews', made an attempt to address some core issues pertaining to empowerment of women supported by facts and figures and individual case studies, the readings contained in this volume put ample light on the concepts, theories practice of women empowerment and development in general and in the context India in general.

Rameshwari Pandya and Sarika Patel (2010) in the book 'Women in the Unorganized Sector of India', deals with the problems of women in the unorganized sector of India. The policies and programmes of the Government to address these problems are also discussed; importantly it includes a case study of women in the embroidery industry of Surat city of the Indian state of Gujarat.

Manvinder Dhallon (2010) in her book 'Economic Empowerment of Women', captures the insights economic empowerment of women in the new millennium, the status of women in the society, and the changing ideologies. This book is a dedicated account of the transition of the Indian women from a home maker to an empowered partner that works at an equal level to its male counterparts to support the family and lead it towards a better lifestyle.

Dr. Rosa K. D. (2010) in her study on 'Empowerment of Women the Impact of Employment', highlights on this important topic re-energises both, management thought and proactive on this subject. It is the critical to have substantive research and discussion on women in the work place.

Rajib Lochan Panigrahy and Sudhansu Sekhar Nayak (2010) in their book entitled 'Women Entrepreneurship' expressed; promoting entrepreneurship among women is certainly a short cut to rapid economic growth and development. Elimination of all forms of gender discrimination is needed and allows women to be the entrepreneur at par with men.

Goutam Patikar and Komal Singh (2010) in their study on 'Scenario of Micro-finance in India' viewed that micro-finance in India is still in its nascent stage. Micro-finance yet remains a powerful tool for development, but it has brought a sea of change in the lives of many in the poor and over-populated country India.

E. A. Narayana and E. V. Laxmi (2011) have made an attempt in their book 'Women Development in India', to highlight many aspect of women development. The important aspect covered in the book includes status of Indian women, women development policies and programmes Institutions Mechanism for women development in India organizational structure functions and programmes of women development organizations perceptions on development organizations.

Pankaj Gupta (2011) in the book entitled 'Studies in Economics of Micro-finance', dealt access to finance by the poor and vulnerable groups is a pre-requisite for a poverty reduction and social cohesion. Providing access to finance is a form of empowerment of the vulnerable groups. The book contains roots of micro-finance, group lending, savings and insurance gender, measuring impact, subsidy and sustainability and managing micro-finance.

Edwin Grandhas and M. Mahalaxmi (2011) in his book 'Micro-finance and Self-Help Groups', made an analysis for an understanding of the micro-finance issues that comprise the subject matter of economic development. The book addresses the linkage of SHGs and micro-finance institutions and the magnitude of the development gap between the rich and the poor in the economy. The study discusses the measurement of poverty, low levels of capital illumination, and the process of structural change in the SHGs.

B. N. Rath (2011) in his book 'Livelihood and Micro-finance', stressed on need for policy interventions to address the rural power. Rural financial intermediation currently constitutes a key development intervention in many poor countries. Yet, the success achieved particularly in countries who implemented such programmes a couple of decades ago notwithstanding, there remain many constraints limiting both the supply and demand in very poor countries like Ethiopia. Experience from over ten years of financial intermediation reveals that good intentions for expansion of supply are having difficulties due to poorly designed regulations and policies, organizational behaviours, the incentive problem, as well as weak capacity of institutions implementing it. Where poverty alleviation constitutes the main development agenda, rural financial regulations and policies tend to have an in-built rationing mechanism, targeting primarily the poorest and the disadvantages, thus often missing others who might also have the demand for it.

B. N. Rath (2011) an analysis has been made in his book 'Micro-credit and Micro-credit Investments', micro-credit belongs to the group of financial service innovations under the term of micro-finance, other services according to micro-finance is micro savings, money transfer vehicles and micro insurance. Micro-credit is an innovation for the developing countries. Micro-credit is a service for poor people that are unemployed, entrepreneurs or farmers who are not bankable. The reason why they are not bankable is the lack of collateral, steady employment, income and a verifiable credit history, because of this reasons they can't even meet the minimal qualifications for an ordinary credit. By helping people with micro-credits it gives them more available choices and opportunities with a reduced risk. It has successfully enabled poor people to start their own business generating or sustain on income and often begin to build up wealth and exit poverty.

B. N. Rath (2011) in his book 'Micro-finance and Risk Management' focused on risk management. A risk is an exposure to the chance of loss. Risks are not inherently bad. Sometimes, it is necessary to take risks to accomplish worthy and meaningful goals. This is especially true in micro-finance where loan officers take risks everyday by lending money to people without credit histories, without business records and often without collateral. One has to take risks to operate a successful micro-finance institution but it is important to take calculated risks. Risk management, or the process of taking calculated risks, reduced the likelihood that a loss will occur and minimizes the scale of the loss should it occur. Risk management includes both the prevention of potential problems and the early detection of actual problems when they occur. Over the past decade, providers of micro-finance have developed an array of models for delivering financial services to the poor that meet the dual criteria of sustainability and outreach.

3 THE SELF-HELP GROUP BANK-LINKAGE MODEL

Drawing lessons from experiment carried out in various parts of the world, particularly in Bangladesh, Sri Lanka, Thailand, Indonesia, Bolivia, Cambodia, Chile and many others, an attempt was made in India to build financial relationship between informal groups of people and formal agencies like banks for catering to the financial requirements of the poor, especially women. After an initial pilot study the RBI setup a working group on NGOs and SHGs. The working group made recommendations for internalisation of the SHG concept as a potential intervention tool in the area of banking with the poor. The RBI was quick to accept the recommendations and advised the banks to consider mainstreaming leading to SHGs as part of their rural credit operations.

The SHG Bank-linkage programme (SBLP) was launched by NABARD in 1991-92 by linking SHGs with banks through a pilot project with the objective of extending formal banking services to the unreached rural poor by evolving a supplementary credit delivery strategy in a cost effective manner has emerged as the largest micro-finance programme in the world in terms of outreach and sustainability. The programme was upgraded to a regular banking programme in 1996. The scheme has been extended to RRBs and co-operative banks. As the formal banking system already has a vast branch network in rural areas, it has perhaps wise to find ways and means to improve the access of rural poor to the existing bank network.

Design Feature of SHG Bank-Linkage

- Enable exclusion of privileged elements.
- Self-selection.
- Focus on women.
- Savings first and credit later.
- Inter group appraisal of needs and/credit prioritization/credit rationing no collaterals (Group cohesion) Group savings serve the purpose.
- Shorter repayment terms.
- Market rate of interest.
- Progressive lending/multiple lending.

Models of Linkage

In India three types of SHG models have emerged.

(i) *Bank-SHG-Members:* In this model the bank itself acts as a self-help group promoting institution (SHIP).

(ii) *Bank-NGO-MFI-SHG-Members:* In this model the bank acts both as cultivator and micro-finance intermediaries.

(iii) *Bank-Facilitating Agency-SHG Members:* Facilitating agencies like NGOs, government agencies, or other community based organizations form groups and are financed by banks.

Among three models, model 2 has become an important alternative to traditional lending. Around 75 per cent of SHGs formed by other agencies are directly financed by banks. Model-1 *i.e.* SHGs formed and financed by banks account 17 per cent of linkage and the third model accounts 8 per cent linkage.

SHG BANK-LINKAGE PROGRAMME IN INDIA

Based on the studies mentioned above, and the results of action research conducted, NABARD developed the SHG-Bank Linkage (SBL) approach as the core strategy that could be used by the banking system in India for increasing their outreach to the poor. The SHG bank linkage programme in India has made rapid strides in recent years. A large number of SHGs linked with the objective of extending formal banking services to the unreached rural poor. During 2005-06 about 6, 20,109 new SHGs were credit linked with banks, while on 31-3-2006, in India the position in respect on cumulative basis is a follows:

- In total 22.38 lakh SHGs got coverage.
- Assistance to 3.30 crore poor families *i.e.*, about 16.50 crore are benefited.
- Cumulative bank loan of Rs. 11395.95 crore.
- About 95 per cent of SHGs are exclusively women group.
- Membership is mainly rural (78%).
- Average bank loan per SHG works out Rs. 50,000.
- Over 95 per cent on time payment of loans.
- 72 per cent finance is made for investment and 28 per cent to meet house hold needs.
- 53 per cent client has used productive activities or assets.
- 70 per cent increase in income is reported for micro-credit supported enterprises.
- 90 per cent clients are in south India.
- MF aims at helping the poor to manage their vulnerability.
- MF aim at increasing social capital by diversifying leadership.
- MF takes up development issues like child labour, environment coiners.
- According to regional spread of bank loan disbursal, the southern region accounted for 54 per cent (highest) of the SHG credit link and central region (including MP) for 12 per cent.

On 31st march 2007, 29.24 lakh SHGs in 587 districts of India have been credit linked to 44500 branches of 50 commercial banks, 352 co-operative banks and 96 RRBs. The cumulative credit provided to SHGs is 18040.74 crore and refinanced by NABARD is Rs. 5446.49 crore. Thus NABARD is playing a pre-eminent role in the Indian MF sector.

NABARD UNDER SHG BANK-LINKAGE PROGRAMME

NABARD has been playing a very important role in the growth of SHG Bank-linkage. During 90s NABARD conducted a series of action research studies. The study revealed that despite having wide network of bank branches the poor continued to remain outside the fold of formal banking system. Thus, began the search for alternative policies, systems, procedures, savings and loan products which would meet the requirements of poor households, especially the women members. Based on the positive and encouraging findings of the studies as also the experimental research project undertaken by NABARD, the basic idea to link formal and informal sectors emanated. Thus, in 1992, NABARD in consultation with RBI initiated the Pilot Project for linking 500 SHGs with banks for improving the access of poor to credit. This could be considered as a landmark development in banking with the poor, as it formed the basis for the emergence of Self-Help Group Banks-Linkage Programme (SHG-BLP), the most successful inclusive growth strategy so far in the Indian economy. The SHG-Bank Linkage has passed through various phases' of pilot testing (1992-95) and expansion (1998 onwards) and metamorphosed into biggest micro-finance movement in the world. The progress in the Bank-Linkage Programme since its inception is given below. (Table 3.1)

As at the end of 2009-10, 69.53 lakh SHGs saving linked with banks having saving of Rs. 6198.71 against 61.21 lakh SHGs having savings of Rs. 5455.62 crore as on 31 March 2009. The above includes 16.94 lakh SGSY groups with savings of Rs. 1292.62 crore which formed 24.4 per cent of total SHGs and 20.85 per cent of total savings.

As at the end of March 2009-10, 48.51 lakh SHGs have been credit linked with outstanding bank loan of Rs. 28038.28 crore against 42.24 lakh SHGs with bank loan outstanding of Rs. 22679.85 as on 31 March 2009, thereby registered a growth rate of 8.71 per cent (No. of SHGs) and 8.08 per cent (Bank loan).

During 2019-10, the bank financed 15.87 lakh SHGs including repeat loans, to the extent of Rs. 14453.30 crore against 16.10 lakh SHGs with bank loan of Rs. 12253.31 crore in 2008-09. Though there is a decline in the number of groups financed during 2009-10, the quantum of loan disbursed has increased indicating that thrust given by banks in increasingly meeting the credit needs of the groups.

Table 3.1: SHG Bank-Linkage (1992-93 to 2009-10)

Year	No. of SHGs Financed	Bank Loan (Rs. Lakh)	No. of Families Assisted	Average Loan per SHG (Rs.)	Average Loan per Family (Rs.)
1992-93	255	30	4335	11765	692
1993-94	365	36	6205	9863	580
1994-95	1502	179	25534	11917	701
1995-96	2635	361	44795	13700	806
1996-97	3841	578	65297	15048	885
1997-98	5719	1192	97223	20843	1226
1998-99	18678	3330	317526	17828	1049
1999-00	81780	13590	1390260	16618	978
2000-01	149050	28789	2533850	19315	1136
2001-02	197653	54554	3360101	27601	1624
2002-03	255882	102231	3754874	26985	1799
2003-04	361731	185550	4586000	36180	2412
2004-05	518173	296180	7774000	42971	2864
2005-06	482598	309613	7238970	64155	4277
2006-07	1105749	657039	15480486	59420	3961
2007-08	1227770	884926	17188780	72076	5148
2008-09	1609586	1225351	22534204	76108	5436
2009-10	1587000	1445330	22218000	91073	6505

Source: NABARD Annual Report.

During 2009-10, the bank financed 1915 MFIs with bank loan of Rs. 5009.09 crore as against 581 MFIs with bank loan of Rs. 3732.33 crore during the previous year. As may be seen there from the numbers of MFIs financed have more than doubled.

1. Nabard Initiatives

During 2009-10, assistance to the tune of Rs. 97.17 lakh benefiting 21348 members/partners has been disbursed towards various promotional initiatives by NABARD.

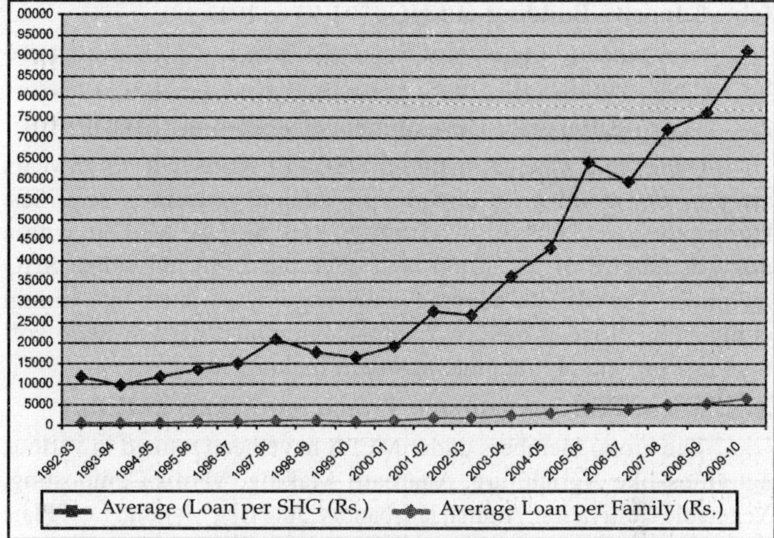

Fig. 3.1: SHG Bank-Linkage (1992-93 to 2009-10)

(a) Training and Capacity Building

NABARD provides financial support by way of grant for the following activities:

- Capacities building of the partner agencies like NGOs, Banks, Government Officials.
- Capacity building of SHG leaders/members.
- Exposure visit to banks/institutions pioneering in micro-finance initiatives.
- Field visits to nearby SHGs for official of Block Level Bankers' Committee.

(i) Grant Assistance

(b) Promotion and linkage SHGs

Self-Help Promoting Institutions (SHIPs) being supported by NABARD include Non-Government Organizations, DCC Banks and Regional Rural Banks. During the year 2009-10, NABARD sanctioned grant assistance of Rs. 79.450 lakh for promotion and linkage of 2190 groups taking the cumulative sanction to Rs. 350.11 lakh for promotion and credit linkage of 25200 groups.

1. Capacity Building of SHGs

Assistance to the tune of Rs. 11.73 lakh to NGOs sanctioned for capacity building of SHGs.

2. Micro-Enterprise Development Programme (MEDP)

Under this scheme, matured SHGs of more than three years are provided training for undertaking income generation activities. During the year 2009-10, NABARD sanctioned 80 MEDPs with a grant assistance of Rs. 21.60 lakh covering 2440 individual SHG members. The MEDPs covered wide range of activities like vermin composting, food products, Zardosi, integrated agro-system, soft toys making, rubber tapping, agarbatti making, etc.

3. Micro-Entrepreneurship Promotion Agency (MEPA)

The group members under MEPA have been trained in various activities like Agriculture, Agarbatti Making, Vermi Composting, Vegetable Cultivation, Animal Husbandry, Jute Bag Making, Leaf Plate Making, Condiments Making, etc.

4. Support for SHG Federations

As a measure to ensure sustenance of SHGs, NABARD initiated a scheme for supporting SHG Federation during 2007-08. The scheme is presently on a model-neutral basis. As on 31 March 2010, NABARD has sanctioned grant assistance of Rs. 12.06 lakh to 18 Community Managed Resource Centres (CMRCs) for supporting 65 Federations covering 1849 SHGs. The SHG Federation can support SHGs with various non-financial services like development training, procurement of input, marketing of products, legal counseling, etc.

5. Scheme for Providing Technology Support to NGOs for Strengthening MIS

NGOs associated with NABARD for promotion of SHGs are provided grant assistance of a maximum of Rs. 50,000 for purchase of computer for strengthening MIS. NABARD provide software and hardware support to NGOs who have promoted a minimum of 250 SHGs. During the year 2009-10, three NGOs with grant assistance of Rs. 1.33 lakh have been supported.

6. Scheme for Rating of MFIs

To enable MFIs/MFOs to leverage funds from banks/financial institutions, a onetime grant assistance of Rs. 3 lakh is provided to

MFIs/MFOs to get them rated through accredited rating agencies. MFIs with minimum loan outstanding of Rs. 50 lakh and maximum of Rs. 10 crore would be eligible. Banks can also avail 100 per cent reimbursement of expenses towards rating of MFIs up to Rs. 3 lakh by way of grant. During the year 2009-10 an amount of Rs. 2.12 lakh was sanctioned to MFIs.

(c) Joint Liability Groups (JLGs)

In order to give focused attention to the needs of mid-segment groups, especially those of landless farmers/share croppers/oral lessees taking up farming and allied activities, there is a need to promote JLGs. Promotion of JLG also helps the farmers to strengthen their collective bargaining power. NABARD has recently formulated guidelines for supporting promotion of JLGs.

(d) Documentation and Dissemination

NABARD has supported development of exclusive software known as NABYUKTI by MYRADA, to facilitate the self-help promoting institutions to have appropriate data base for effective monitoring. NABARD has been distributing the software free of cost to SHPIs wanting to develop database on the functioning of their SHGs.

(e) SHG Bank-Linkage Award

Public recognition of excellent performance motivates the bankers/NGOs and enables to sustain the interest in the SHG Bank-Linkage Programme. In pursuit of this, NABARD over the years has instituted State Level Awards for the best performance under the SHG Bank-Linkage Programme to facilitate and motivate the stakeholders .The awards are based on specific parameters such as ratio of SHG portfolio to overall loan portfolio, average per group finance, average per branch SHG credit linked etc.

(*ii*) Financial Support

(a) General Refinance Scheme

NABARD refinance is available to commercial banks, DCC banks, and RRBs for financing SHGs:

- *Quantum*: 100 per cent loan disbursed or loan outstanding, whichever is less.

- *Interest Rate*: Prevailing interest rate at the time of release of finance to banks.
- *Repayment Period*: 3 to 10 years.

(b) Refinance Scheme for Financing Matured SHGs for Farm Production and Investment Activities

NABARD, in addition to the existing refinance facility for SHGs, has opened a separate line of finance for banks for financing farm production and investment activities through matured SHGs. Term loan and cash credit limits given by the banks for a period of five years to matured SHGs exclusively for farm production and investment activities covering agriculture sector and allied activities will be eligible under the scheme.

(c) Support to MFIs

Realising the need and potential of MFIs and the importance attached to their role by the GOI, NABARD has been supporting MFIs to further accelerate the availability of financial services in rural areas. The support from NABARD to MFIs is available in the following forms:

Scheme for Capital Support to MFIs

The scheme was introduced during the year 2006-07. This scheme has been introduced with the objective of encouraging alternative micro credit innovations. The capital/equity support to MFIs is provided so as to enable them to leverage capital/equity for accessing commercial and other funds from bank, for providing financial services at an affordable cost to the poor and to enable MFIs to achieve sustainability in their credit operations over a period of 3-5 years.

Revolving Fund Assistance to MFIs for on-lending to SHGs

The refinance fund assistance support is aimed at facilitating the supported agencies to provide funds to the disadvantaged and excluded persons at an affordable cost. With a view to have a balanced growth of the MFI sector, NABARD also provides capital support/ revolving fund assistance to the start up MFIs who are between 6 months to 2 years old. MFIs having the effective interest rate of more than 25 per cent per annum to the ultimate clients are not considered for support under the above scheme.

Micro-Insurance

It is a provision of insurance facilities to the low income group, for enhancing the ability of the poor to deal with various risks in the lives.

Monitoring and Co-ordination Guidance

The for a like BLBC, DLCC at district level and SLBC at State level have been given the task of reviewing the progress and co-ordinating the efforts, sorting out operational issues related to SHG Bank-Linkage Programme.

SHG BANK-LINKAGE PROGRAMME IN KARNATAKA

The self-help movement is deep-rooted in southern States and Karnataka has been in forefront in terms of promotion and credit linkage and has initiated many innovations in furthering the growth of SHG movement in the country. The fresh SHGs formed and credit linked (including indirect linkage) during the year 2009-10 were 74,208 and 57,975 respectively taking the cumulative SHGs formed and credit linked in the State to 5,94,117 and 5,30,210 respectively as on 31 March 2010. The average loan per SHG has risen from Rs. 70,797 during 2008-09 to Rs. 1, 08,971 during 2009-10.

Micro-finance Profile in Karnataka

Conducive atmosphere for the spread of micro-finance exists in the state. Many NGOs/SHPIs have been promoting self help groups. Most of the major commercial banks as also the Regional Rural Bank and the – District Central Co-operative Banks are playing the role of 'Credit Purveyor' to SHGs. Government department of Women and Child Development Department (WCDD) is promoting 'Stree Shakti' groups. The micro-finance profile of the state is as under: (Table 3.2)

The progress of SHG-bank-linkage scheme in Karnataka shows that the number of groups increased over a period of time from 519,909 in March, 2009 to 594,117 on March, 2010 and the bank loan mobilized under the scheme has witnessed a phenomenal rise from 4,023.96 crores in March, 2009 to 5,257.51 crores on March, 2010. The district wise details of SHGs in Karnataka is presented in Table 3.3 and Table 3.4.

Table 3.2: Salient Features of SHG Bank-Linkage Programme in Karnataka

Sl. No.	Particulars	As on 31 March 2009	During 2009-10	As on 31 March 2010
1.	No. of SHGs promoted	519,909	74,208	594,117
2.	No. of SHGs credit linked (New Groups)	472,235	57,975	530,210
3.	No. of SHGs financed (new and repeat groups) Indirect linkage through MFIs		115,566 45,864	
4.	Amount of Bank loan availed (Rs. crore) Amount of MFI loans availed (Rs. crore)	4,023.96	1233.55 286.67	5,257.51
5.	No. of families covered under the programme (lakh)	72.79	8.05	80.84
6.	Percentage of women SHGs Average loan per SHG (Rs.) during 2009-10	70,797	108,571	Over 90%
7.	No. of participating banks			73
8.	No. of bank branches lending to SHGs (including PACS)			8,372
9.	No. of NGOs participating in the programme directly/indirectly			350
10.	Amount of NABARD refinance (Rs. crore)	796.47	224.64	1,021.11

Source: NABARD Annual Report.

Table 3.3 presents the details regarding the number of groups formed, category of members in the state of Karnataka. Table 3.3 shows that the highest SHGs formed in Belgaum district and Kolar district registered lowest SHGs in Karnataka. Belgaum district has 13398 and Kolar district has 3928 with a membership of 212980 and 58883 respectively. Of the total members, 20.25 per cent (383,710) belong to SC category, 8.26 per cent (156,533) are ST members, 7.34 per cent are pertaining to minority community and remaining 64.15 per cent (12,54,053) are belonging to other category. The progress of SHGs in Karnataka is indicated in Table 3.4.

Table 3.3: Progress of SHGs in Karnataka (July 2008)

Sl. No.	District	Total No. SHGs A	Total No. of Women SHG Members SC B	Total No. of Women SHG Members ST C	Total No. of Women SHG Members Minority D	Total No. of Women SHG Members Others E	Total No. of Women SHG Members All Category F	Total No. of Groups having Bank Linkages G
1	2	3	4	5	6	7	8	9
1.	Bangalore	2990	13577	1684	1762	33771	50794	2979
2.	Bangalore Rural	3137	10963	4838	3352	19354	38507	2645
3.	Bagalkot	3839	11391	4541	4561	42010	62483	3460
4.	Belgaum	13398	29112	20283	20283	143302	212980	9685
5.	Bellary	4870	13327	9064	7064	30347	59802	4138
6.	Bidar	2739	10646	3537	3537	24451	42171	2112
7.	Bijapur	3603	4968	702	2085	10995	18750	2505
8.	Chamarajnagar	3700	14817	5178	1044	38682	59721	3096
9.	Chikkamanglur	2918	7678	1853	3137	23141	35809	2634
10.	Chikkaballapur	4547	14413	7586	1006	32760	55765	4163
11.	Chitradurga	4733	12788	10693	1770	31184	56435	4335
12.	Davangere	4430	13129	7854	3076	30624	54633	3583

Contd...

1	2	3	4	5	6	7	8	9
		A	B	C	D	E	F	G
13.	Dakshina Kannada	3638	6372	5236	3588	9505	51297	32948
14.	Dharwad	2704	5155	3026	6630	34266	49077	1902
15.	Gadag	3041	5393	2961	6529	25742	40625	2361
16.	Gulbarga	8500	36720	7350	12963	71141	128174	5967
17.	Hassan	6042	16748	2611	1738	74772	95869	5246
18.	Haveri	4260	11693	8285	7914	42166	70058	3249
19.	Kodagu	928	3194	1703	2009	8853	15259	774
20.	Kolar	3928	20126	3905	4708	30144	58883	2220
21.	Koppal	2640	9377	6191	2980	22622	41170	2210
22.	Mandya	6214	14721	546	2877	83908	101652	5553
23.	Mysore	6153	24773	9766	4127	77487	116153	4180
24.	Raichur	4760	11359	9702	7725	27965	56751	3342
25.	Ramnagar	4407	14596	1442	1368	56861	74267	3709
26.	Shimoga	3880	10116	2121	3326	32895	43458	3604
27.	Tumkur	9544	32516	12871	3456	77611	131454	8259
28.	Udupi	2675	1638	3347	3005	34772	42762	2461
29.	Uttar Kannada	1777	2364	673	1399	20176	24612	1476

Source: Women and Children Development Department, Bangalore July-2008 Report.

Table 3.4: Progress of SHGs in Karnataka (July 2008)

Sl. No.	District	Savings Accumulated (in crores)	No. of Groups Loan Taken from the Bank	Total Loan Amount taken from Bank (in crores)	Revolving Fund Released from Bank (in crores)	Loan Amount Distributed by SHG (in crores)	Total Repayment Amount to SHG (in crores)	Total Repayment amount to Bank (in crores)
1	2	3	4	5	6	7	8	9
		A	B	C	D	E	F	G
1.	Bangalore	26.66	2979	41.97	1.445	58.62	53.42	37.18
2.	Bangalore Rural	17.99	2645	23.73	1.5685	64.43	46.01	33.27
3.	Bagalkot	19.19	3460	15.11	1.9195	29.75	23.23	11.42
4.	Belgaum	44.43	9685	37.94	6.0699	57.74	48.18	31.95
5.	Bellary	22.25	4138	23.35	2.0485	32.83	25.61	20.66
6.	Bidar	15.34	2112	13.63	1.3695	35.59	29.03	12.87
7.	Bijapur	13.06	2505	10.9	1.8015	26.58	19.05	8.83
8.	Chamarajnagar	0.16	3096	25.59	1.8580	55.90	41.09	21.26
9.	Chikkamanglur	15.39	2634	13.47	1.4590	52.22	48.38	14.11
10.	Chikkaballapur	26.24	4163	15.18	2.2735	55.35	47.16	39.36
11.	Chitradurga	25.73	4335	27.25	2.8685	65.49	48.65	21.11
12.	Davangere	22.52	3583	25.86	2.2150	46.25	30.06	19.43

Contd…

1	2	3	4	5	6	7	8	9
		A	B	C	D	E	F	G
13.	Dakshina Kannada	18.66	32948	49.05	1.8190	67.57	52.20	36.46
14.	Dharwad	11.07	1902	9.75	1.3520	10.74	9.20	4.94
15.	Gadag	7.25	2361	8.53	1.5205	19.37	10.54	5.88
16.	Gulbarga	42.26	5967	29.76	4.2500	115.26	79.98	31.01
17.	Hassan	30.08	5246	17.20	3.0250	138.25	106.31	40.28
18.	Haveri	19.98	3249	23.00	2.1300	93.91	59.60	19.62
19.	Kodagu	6.52	774	6.46	0.464	28.18	26.64	12.44
20.	Kolar	15.15	2220	14.33	1.964	44.22	41.19	16.90
21.	Koppal	9.40	2210	8.55	1.230	16.56	9.89	5.85
22.	Mandya	44.58	5553	36.42	3.107	131.69	107.85	45.44
23.	Mysore	27.53	4180	27.15	3.0765	84.12	74.10	38.15
24.	Raichur	14.87	3342	10.94	2.3800	27.33	13.07	6.47
25.	Ramnagar	23.82	3709	40.61	2.2035	88.53	63.34	54.36
26.	Shimoga	17.09	3604	30.81	1.9400	75.78	72.73	25.26
27.	Tumkur	42.20	8259	62.66	4.7745	130.84	104.07	76.14
28.	Udupi	24.67	2461	31.36	1.3375	56.66	55.55	33.21
29.	Uttar Kannada	7.95	1476	6.10	0.8835	33.50	29.68	7.44
	Total	**611.75**	**105242**	**685.375**	**65.00**	**1739.59**	**1372.63**	**729.37**

Source: Women and Children Development Department, Bangalore July-2008 Report.

Table 3.4 indicates the accumulated savings, bank loan availed, revolving fund released, loan distributed by SHGs, repayment of loan to banks and repayment of loan to SHGs in various districts of Karnataka. It is revealed from the table that the accumulated savings up to July, 2008 amounted to Rs. 611.75 crores. Mandya district registered highest saving followed by Belgaum, Gulbarga and Tumkur districts. Out of 1, 30,000 groups 1,05,242 groups are linked to banks with loan of Rs. 685.375 crores. As on July 2008, the SHGs received revolving fund of Rs. 65 crores and the loan disbursed by the SHGs to the members Rs. 1739.59 crores. The members of the groups have made repayment of loan to SHGs to the extent of Rs. 1372.63 crores and to the banks Rs. 729.37 crores. The agency wise-linkage of SHGs in Karnataka from 1995-2010 is shown in Table 3.5.

Table 3.5: Credit Linkage by Various Agencies (Cumulative)

Year (as on 31 March)	Commercial Banks*		RRBs*		Co-operative	
	No of SHGs Linked	Bank Loan (Rs. Lakh)	No of SHGs Linked	Bank Loan (Rs. Lakh)	No of SHGs Linked	Bank Loan (Rs. Lakh)
1995	316	42.85	340	46.10	–	–
1996	1034	143.00	658	91.03	–	–
1997	1425	206.00	1022	186.65	5	0.50
1998	2008	297.27	1528	314.57	54	13.50
1999	2974	473.61	2417	513.34	201	68.25
2000	4829	1017.60	4735	1000.20	1046	212.30
2001	6395	1452.00	8334	1647.70	3890	576.80
2002	14425	2426.24	13279	3021.70	9328	1951.70
2003	20987	4539.58	23473	6048.29	17718	3973.05
2004	35912	10227.38	38631	10947.28	29323	7346.63
2005	54812	20210.36	62732	21973.31	45652	12991.16
2006	78520	36420.85	83383	38413.39	63025	24600.61
2007	139341	85925.91	99931	55718.50	78364	39429.31
2008	198262	134572.32	117038	82387.80	96616	64560.04
2009	223853	201736.77	136690	113339.14	111692	87319.62
2010	256796	263095.00	149097	147144.00	124317	115512.00

* = Both Direct and Indirect Linkage.

The role of commercial banks as compared to RRBs and co-operative banks in participating in the SHG bank linkage has been greater. Table 3.5 reveals that the overall credit flow from all the three agencies *viz*. Commercial Banks, RRBs and Co-operative Banks raised in Karnataka. Commercial banks have disbursed loans amounting to Rs. 263096 lakh, constituting around 50 per cent of the loan disbursed during the year. The RRBs have disbursed Rs. 147144 lakh. Karnataka Vikas Grameena Bank and Pragati Grameena Bank have made significant contribution to the programme. Cooperative banks have disbursed loans amounting to Rs. 115512 lakh during the period. Reports depicts that the role of RRB and cooperative banks has been continuously increasing in recent years.

AGENCIES INVOLVED IN MICRO-FINANCE IN BELGAUM DIVISION OF KARNATAKA

Stree Shakti

Karnataka Government through its women and child Development Department continued its mission of empowering rural poor women in seven districts of the study area through its through its Stree Shakti programme. WCDD has facilitated promotion 32622 Stree Shakti Groups as on 31 March 2009. The state government in co-ordination with NABARD has been striving to strengthen the groups in the region. The state government has allowed interest subversion to co-operatives for ensuring access of loans by SHGs at a low rate of 4 per cent interest per annum. The State Government has also for the year 2010-11 extended the scheme for interest subversion of 6 per cent to nationalized banks in respect of loan intended to women SHGs promoted with the assistance of government department.

Banks

Banks are playing significant role in providing micro credit to the poor in the region. The commercial banks disbursement of loan constitutes around 50 per cent of the loan disbursed in the area under study further commercial banks have also been reaching SHGs through MFIs and nearly 70 to 80 per cent of the loans of MFIs to SHGs are through borrowings from commercial banks.

During 2009-10 RRBs have made a significant disbursement. The Karnataka Vikas Grameen Bank is the leading RRB of the region.

Co-operative banks in this region make significant contribution in micro credit segment. The segment is monitored by exclusive Nodal officers positioned in each DCCB and reviewed on a quarterly basis.

Micro-finance Institutions

Micro-finance institutions are quite active in Karnataka as well as in Belgaum division of Karnataka. About 48 MFIs are active in the State, but their activities have not so for been authentically documented. Recent emergence of Association of Karnataka micro-finance institution (AKMI) is expected to facilitate documentation of the MFIs.

Non-government Organizations (NGOs)

The NGOs have played a very cruel role in SHG Bank-Linkage Programme movement in the region. The NGOs not only promote SHGs but are actively involved in building the capacities of the SHGs and inculcating financial discipline. They have remained a crucial link between the SHGs on the one hand and development functionaries, including the government on the other. The NGOs are working with NABARD as SHIP partners. Shree Kshetra Dharmasthala Rural Development Project (SKDRDP), Mysore Resettlement and Development Agency (MYRADA) are the two prominent NGOs of Karnataka recognised by NABARD as the NGO micro-finance institution. Sangamitra Rural Financial Services, initiative for Development Foundation etc., are the other NGO working activity in Karnataka. Among these SKDRDP has taken initiatives in 26 of the 30 districts of Karnataka through its community development projects. The SKDRDP is activity engaged in intensive fight against poverty, ignorance, literacy, alcoholic abuse, gender discrimination, and greed and money power in the districts. The SKDRDP is very active in three coastal districts. Among the three coastal districts Uttar Kannada district is coming under the preview of this region.

NABARD

Right from the pilot Phase NABARD is actively involved in SHG-BPL movements in this region. The NABARD has been facilitating interaction among the stockholders to address various issues relating to up scaling SHG-BPL Movement.

Swarna Jayanthi Gram Swarojagar Yojana (SGSY)

The Government of India implemented many poverty alleviation programmes since independence but the impact found to be limited. By merging more number of poverty alleviation programmes the government was launched SGSY in 1999. The objective of SGSY is to assist rural people who are living below poverty line to take up self-employment providing the bank credit and subsidy. It is a programme run jointly by central and state government in 75:75 bases.

Micro-finance in Belgaum Division OFI Karnataka

Mumbai Karnataka Region known as Belgaum revenue division in the state of Karnataka was remained with the Bombay presidency till the state re-organization till November 1956. Therefore, this region is recognised by the people of Karnataka as Mumbai Karnataka region. The micro-finance programmes is deep rooted in this region. The Government of Karnataka, NGOs, MFIs, DCCBs, PACS commercial banks and RRBs continued to play a very significant role in the promotion of SHGs in the region. The year wise formation of SHGs in Belgaum division of Karnataka are shown below.

Table 3.6: District-wise SHGs Formed in Belgaum Division of Karnataka (1999-2000 to 2005-06)

Name of the Districts	1999-2000	2000-01	2001-02	2002-03	2003-04	2004-05	2005-06	Total
Bagalkot	14	69	310	381	576	756	727	2833
Belgaum	128	308	434	937	1480	2766	3622	9675
BIjapur	160	260	326	550	518	1082	1063	3959
Dharwad	287	494	380	366	795	773	1485	4580
Gadag	20	68	182	172	527	732	1268	2969
Haveri	29	121	287	321	618	1259	2162	4797
Uttar Kannada	34	83	168	743	982	1267	1430	4707
Total	**672**	**1403**	**2087**	**3470**	**5496**	**8635**	**11757**	**33520**

Source: SHG Bank-Linkage Programme me in Karnataka 2005-06.

Table 3.6 reveals the total number of groups formed in the region from the year 1999-2000 to 2005-06. The highest number of groups formed in Belgaum district *i.e.* 9675 followed by Haveri, Dharwad and Uttar Kannada Districts respectively whereas, Bagalkot district registered only 2833 groups during this period. The progress of SHGs in Karnataka is shown in Table 3.7.

Table 3.7: District-wise Bank Loan Disbursed to SHGs in Belgaum Division of Karnataka (1999-2000 to 2005-06) (in Crore)

Name of the Districts	1999-2000	2000-01	2001-02	2002-03	2003-04	2004-05	2005-06	Total
Bagalkot	01.69	04.65	41.77	35.79	197.90	264.98	485.70	1032.48
Belgaum	15.41	36.70	117.09	314.94	619.90	1097.39	2529.00	4730.43
Bijapur	19.27	30.98	74.05	207.60	173.30	469.10	645.20	1619.50
Dharwad	34.56	58.86	95.98	110.20	208.90	442.52	1008.80	1959.82
Gadag	02.41	08.10	53.99	41.80	·116.90	250.68	777.00	1250.98
Haveri	03.49	14.42	74.69	32.10	194.40	578.29	1328.90	2226.29
Uttar Kannada	04.09	09.89	77.12	79.60	433.60	566.01	1007.30	2177.61
Total	**80.92**	**163.60**	**534.69**	**822.03**	**1944.90**	**3668.97**	**7781.90**	**14997.11**

Source: SHG Bank-Linkage Programme me in Karnataka 2005-06.

It is observed from Table 3.7 that the over a period of time the loan disbursement has been considerably increased in Belgaum division of Karnataka. In 2005-06 banks have disbursed to SHGs amounting to Rs. 2529.00 crores in Belgaum district and banks have made a significant disbursement and disbursed Rs. 1328 crores in Haveri district. The disbursement of loans in Dharwad and Uttar Kannada districts amounting to Rs. 1008.80 and 1007.30 crores respectively. The bans have disbursed an amount of Rs. 777.00 crores, Rs. 645.20 crores and Rs. 485.70 crores in Gadag, Bijapur and Bagalkot districts respectively.

Micro-finance programme through self-help groups has been effective in making positive socio-economic change to all the members. Access to bank credit enables the members of the group to invest the money in income-generating activities that would in turn accelerate the economic development. Under the globalised scenario it is all the more important that the group finance be encouraged. A significant development has been taking place in SHG bank-linkage programme due to the growing involvement of local and state governments and various banks. These developments have made a greater socio-economic implications on the rural poor especially women. The economic impact of micro-finance through SHGs is depicted in the IV chapter.

4 ECONOMIC IMPACT OF MICRO-FINANCING THROUGH SHGS

Micro-finance practice in India has much to offer to the rural poor especially the women. Over 90 per cent of the outreach of Micro-finance services to women. It has made a significant contribution towards improving financial access to the weaker sections. India has been experiencing micro-credit in the form of SHGs as a part of formal credit delivery system. Micro-credit through SHGs becomes a ladder for the poor to bring them economically sound. The impact of Micro-finance programme through SHGs has been effective. The SHGs provide income opportunities and financial returns to the members. It creates saving habits and enhances self-confidence of the members. Self-help groups enable the members the spirit of entrepreneurship and increases the employment opportunities. The regular pooled savings provide a sense of security to the members and the created credit fund help them in availing loans for consumption and other purposes. This is expected to have a positive impact on their well-being. The loans availed from SHGs or from banks enable the members to improve their agriculture, dairying and business which are expected to contribute to employment generation, income increase and asset creation. Access to credit benefit the members by improving their living standard and improving the infrastructure such as lighting, storage, transport of members etc.

The SHG's create a common fund by contributing their small savings. The group rotates money to needy members for various purposes at specified interest rates. As the repayment is cent-per cent and re-cycling is fast the saving amount increases rapidly owing to the accumulation of interest. The saving habit help the members to escape from clutches of money lenders. This also helps the rural women to stand on their own feet and build confidence. SHG programme paved the way to rural poor to approach the banks for credit. Government of India having realised the power and potential of SHG approach in alleviating the poverty has started mobilizing the poor women into SHGs. The recent studies on development issues endorsed aptly that, sustainable development can be made possible by making women on equally important paradigm of the development process. Hence, more stress has been given on the empowerment of women particularly rural women by our planers. Lot of policy changes have been made in this filed. SHG's bank linkage programme has made a significant change in the socio-economic life of the households. In this background an attempt has been made in this chapter to assess the performance of the SHGs and the role played by the banks in the rural poor especially women in the study area.

Economic Impact

SHG Bank-linkage programme, in the last two decades provide as a powerful tool to uplift the socio-economic conditions of the rural poor. During 2009-10 the programme has reached to linking 69.5 lakh (Cumulative) saving linked SHGs and 48.5 Lakh (Cumulative) credit linked SHGs and thus about 9.7 crore households are covered under this programme. This indicates that micro-finance programme has become the common vehicle in the development process. The objectives of the chapter is to assess the performance of SHGs and their role in financial service delivery and to analyse the banks performance in improving the income, savings and assets of the poor in Belgaum division of Karnataka state. The analysis is mainly focused on socio-economic characteristics of the members of the SHG, thrift, economic activities pursued with bank credit, details of credit activities with own funds and repayment of loans. An analysis of banks in the area under study has also been made by using various parameters such as loaning to SHGs, utilisation of loan by SHGs, recovery of loan from SHGs, Training of SHGs and impact of bank finance on the SHGs.

Socio-economic Characteristics of the Members of the Groups

Age

It is an established fact that age plays a dominant role in shaping a personality of an individual. The age factor is inter-related with the ability to learn, group and retain. Level of participation in different walks of life and holding of several responsibilities are determined to a great extent by age. The stages of life cycle of women are especially affected by the age span. Thus, the purpose of age span divided into five groups as: 10-20, 21-30, 31-40, 41-50, and 51 above years. The age-wise distribution of SHGs members has been obtained to understand their qualitative and quantitative contributions to their groups. (*See table 4.1 on next page*)

Table 4.1 shows that major proportion of the sample SHG members of the study area fall in the age group of 31-40 years followed by the members in the age group of 21-30 years, 41-50 years respectively and majority of the respondents are female. This shows that the members between 21 to 50 years are more prone to joining SHGs and even out of these, the bigger section of the members hail from age group of 31-40 years.

This might be because of the age at the marriage is low in rural areas, and here women have passed through the major phases of getting married, child bearing and initial child rearing by the age of 30 years. In the age group between 31-40 years women have children who are school going, sharing household and other responsibilities or have to be married. Thus instead of pressure of time, women in this state have pressing financial needs and so are inclined towards joining SHGs. Beyond this age group, the percentage of women associating with SHGs falls down as they are free from almost all the major financial responsibilities and do not have much motivation to get connect with such credit links.

Sex

The distribution of study samples by sex is indicated in the Table 4.2. (*See table on page 73*)

Table 4.1: Age-wise Distribution of the SHG Members

Districts	Total	10-20				21-30			
		Male	%	Female	%	Male	%	Female	%
Bagalkot	1367	0	0.0	46	3.4	8	0.6	397	29.0
Belgaum	1793	0	0.0	31	1.7	40	2.2	363	20.2
Bijapur	2015	0	0.0	86	4.3	16	0.8	637	31.6
Dharwad	1671	0	0.0	41	2.5	24	1.4	414	24.8
Gadag	3151	0	0.0	120	3.8	24	0.8	765	24.3
Haveri	1076	0	0.0	27	2.5	8	0.7	262	24.3
Uttar Kannada	1458	0	0.0	50	3.4	8	0.5	442	30.3
Total	**12531**	**0**	**0.0**	**401**	**3.2**	**128**	**1.0**	**3280**	**26.2**

Districts	31-40				41-50				50+			
	Male	%	Female	%	Male	%	Female	%	Male	%	Female	%
Bagalkot	22	1.6	664	48.6	12	0.9	203	14.9	0	0.0	15	1.1
Belgaum	60	3.3	1015	56.6	37	2.1	247	13.8	0	0.0	0	0.0
Bijapur	46	2.3	911	45.2	19	0.9	279	13.8	0	0.0	21	1.0
Dharwad	36	2.2	853	51.0	22	1.3	269	16.1	0	0.0	12	0.7
Gadag	52	1.7	1511	48.0	46	1.5	573	18.2	0	0.0	60	1.9
Haveri	12	1.1	599	55.7	8	0.7	157	14.6	0	0.0	3	0.3
Uttar Kannada	18	1.2	687	47.1	8	0.5	214	14.7	0	0.0	31	2.1
Total	**246**	**2.0**	**6240**	**49.8**	**152**	**1.2**	**1942**	**15.5**	**0**	**0.0**	**142**	**1.1**

Table 4.2: Distribution of Study Samples by Sex

Districts	Male	%	Female	%	Total	%
Bagalkot	42	3.07	1325	96.93	1367	10.91
Belgaum	137	7.64	1656	92.36	1793	14.31
Bijapur	81	4.02	1934	95.98	2015	16.08
Dharwad	82	4.91	1589	95.09	1671	13.33
Gadag	122	3.87	3029	96.13	3151	25.15
Haveri	28	2.60	1048	97.40	1076	8.59
Uttar Kannada	34	2.33	1424	97.67	1458	11.64
Total	**526**	**4.20**	**12005**	**95.80**	**12531**	**100.00**

Table 4.2 Indicates that more than 95 per cent of respondent are female. Out of total 12531 respondents 12005 (95.80%) were women. Gadag district has the highest respondents followed by Bijapur and Belgaum district. The total numbers of female respondents in Haveri was least *i.e.* 1076. In the male category Belgaum district has the highest members and Gadag district stands second followed by Bijapur and Bagalkot districts. Haveri district stands in the last place. Where as in the female category, Gadag district has 3029 respondents followed by Bijapur district *i.e.* 1934 respondents. The Haveri district has a least of 1048 women respondents selected.

Education

Education is again one such important factors which affects the attitudes and shapes the personality of individuals in a positive manner. Besides, enhancing information and awareness level, education is an important ingredient for social and economic development. The members have little access to education due to social, economic, cultural and situational reasons. The mental abilities improved through formal education might lead to qualitative involvement in the SHG management, banking functions and income-generation. (*See table 4.3 on next page*)

Table 4.3 Shows that 59.01 per cent of the respondent of the study area have no education, 9.08 per cent of the members have an education up to primary level, whereas 18.98 per cent of the respondents are educated up to secondary level and 11.44 per cent of members have an education up to higher secondary level.

Table 4.3: Distribution of Study Samples by Education Status

Districts	No. Education		Primary		Secondary		Higher Secondary and PUC		College	
	Nos	%	Nos	%	Nos	%	Nos	%	Nos	%
Bagalkot	753	55.08	125	9.14	313	22.90	165	12.07	11	0.81
Belgaum	1204	67.15	91	5.08	274	15.28	167	9.31	57	3.18
Bijapur	1114	55.29	215	10.67	381	18.91	294	14.59	11	0.54
Dharwad	986	59.00	169	10.12	296	17.71	184	11.02	36	2.16
Gadag	1913	60.71	265	8.41	566	17.96	367	11.65	40	1.27
Haveri	678	63.01	81	7.53	204	18.96	96	8.92	17	1.58
Uttar Kannada	747	51.23	192	13.17	339	23.25	161	11.05	19	1.30
Total	**7395**	**59.01**	**1138**	**9.08**	**2373**	**18.94**	**1434**	**11.44**	**191**	**1.53**

Out of total members, only 1.54 per cent of members have finished degree from the universities. It is indicated from the Table 4.3 that majority of the members of the SHG in the study are illiterates that hurdles in active participation in group work.

Marital Status

Marriage is considered to be a social obligation in the India society. The status of the married person is regarded high and thus it influences more on the people. Its influence is much more in rural areas. Involvement attitude, awareness and decision-making factors are more associated with marriage. The marital status of the respondents in the area under study is shown in Table 4.4.

Table 4.4 Shows that more than 70 per cent of the members of the SHGs were found married in all the districts except Haveri and Bagalkot.

BPL and APL Membership

The SGSY programme and the SHG approach are formed to address the poor in the rural areas. The basic task of group formation begins with the identification of poorest sections in fact, of the persons living below poverty line. The percentage of BPL and APL membership in SHGs are shown below. (Table 4.5)

Table 4.4: Showing the Marital Status of the Respondents

Districts	Married	%	Unmarried	%	Total	%
Bagalkot	926	67.74	441	32.26	1367	100.00
Belgaum	1256	70.05	537	29.95	1793	100.00
Bijapur	1489	73.90	526	26.10	2015	100.00
Dharwad	1178	70.50	495	29.50	1671	100.00
Gadag	2217	70.36	934	29.64	3151	100.00
Haveri	692	64.31	384	35.69	1076	100.00
Uttar Kannada	1025	70.30	433	29.70	1458	100.00
Total	**8783**	**70.09**	**3748**	**29.91**	**12531**	**100.00**

Table 4.5: Percentages of BPL and APL Membership in SHGs

Districts	BPL	%	APL	%
Bagalkot	862	63.06	505	36.94
Belgaum	775	43.22	1018	56.78
Bijapur	1402	69.58	613	30.42
Dharwad	898	53.74	773	46.26
Gadag	1870	59.35	1281	40.65
Haveri	644	59.85	432	40.15
Uttar Kannada	935	64.13	523	35.87
Total	**7386**	**58.94**	**5145**	**41.06**

Table 4.5 shows that 7386 members belong to BPL group and 5145 members hails from APL category. Around 70 per cent of the respondents of Bijapur district belong to BPL category. Uttar Kannada and Bagalkot districts have 64.13 per cent and 63.06 per cent respectively. The BPL membership was found to be 59.85 per cent in Haveri district and it was 59.35 per cent in Gadag district. The percentage of BPL membership of Dharwad district was 53.74 and the percentage recorded low in case of Belgaum district. It is known from the Table 4.5 that majority of the members of the SHGs in the study area belong to poor section.

Occupation

The family occupation of the individuals decides the economic condition as well as the social status. The main occupation profile of the respondents is given below. (Table 4.6)

Table 4.6: Distribution of Study Samples by Occupation

Districts	Tailoring	%	Labour	%	House wife	%	Dairy	%	Business	%	Agriculture	%
Bagalkot	116	8.50	545	39.87	107	7.84	54	3.92	366	26.80	179	13.07
Belgaum	86	4.79	494	27.54	118	6.59	11	0.60	472	26.35	612	34.13
Bijapur	176	8.73	889	44.10	106	5.24	88	4.37	563	27.95	193	9.61
Dharwad	102	6.08	600	35.91	175	10.50	74	4.42	397	23.76	323	19.34
Gadag	160	5.07	1204	38.21	282	8.96	151	4.78	799	25.37	555	17.61
Haveri	66	6.14	434	40.35	76	7.02	18	1.75	293	27.19	189	17.54
Uttar Kannada	145	9.94	580	39.77	94	6.43	77	5.26	426	29.24	136	9.36
Total	**863**	**6.89**	**4781**	**38.15**	**956**	**7.63**	**483**	**3.85**	**3323**	**26.52**	**2125**	**16.96**

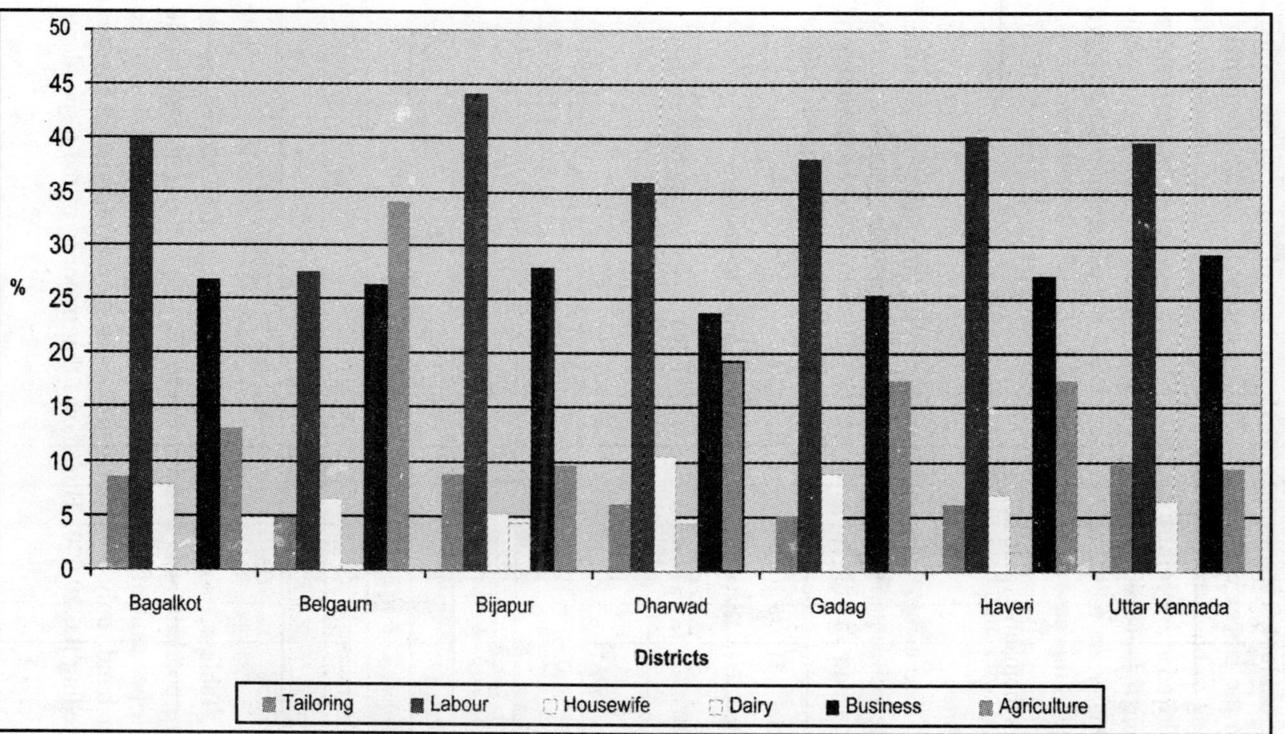

Fig. 4.1: Distribution of Study Samples by Occupation

Table 4.6 shows that 38.15 per cent of the respondents hail from the labour class; while 26.52 per cent of the SHG members belong to business class and 16.46 per cent of the respondents are employed in agriculture whereas only 7.63 per cent of the respondents belong to housewife category. The respondents belonging to tailoring and dairy are 6.89 and 3.85 per cents respectively. The Chi-Square value in this case is 73.1074 and Pearson's R is 0.0000 indicating a significant relationship between occupations and economic conditions of the SHG members in the area under study.

Income

The income from all sources decides the economic status of the respondents. This determines the consumption level, standard of living and saving capacity of the members. The distribution of respondents according to income of the study area is given below. (Table 4.7)

Table 4.7: Distribution of Study Samples by Income

Districts	Below 10,000	%	10,000 to 20,000	%	Above 20,000	%
Bagalkot	529	39.10	790	58.39	34	2.51
Belgaum	370	21.01	1180	67.01	211	11.98
Bijapur	866	44.69	1036	53.46	36	1.86
Dharwad	597	36.56	922	56.46	114	6.98
Gadag	1271	40.83	1707	54.83	135	4.34
Haveri	329	31.67	658	63.33	52	5.00
Uttar Kannada	648	45.51	733	51.47	43	3.02
Total	**4610**	**37.60**	**7026**	**57.30**	**625**	**5.10**
Chi-square = 499.1940, P = 0.0000, S						

Table 4.7 shows that the annual income of 57.30 per cent of the respondents was found between Rs. 10,000 and 20,000, while 37.60 per cent of the respondents earn below Rs. 10,000. On the other hand, only 5.10 per cent of the members have an income exceeding Rs. 20,000. This shows that majority of the respondents

fall into a low income group. The Chi-Square value is 499.1940 and Pearson's R is 0.0000 showing a significant relationship between income of the members and economic status.

Capital Resources

The most popular entry point in SHG is saving. Savings, besides inculcating the habit of thrift, encourage the development of a long-term vision. It helps in developing confidence in members. Management of group savings by the members themselves also helps them develop capacity in handling of money and prioritising of needs of different members. The group should decide voluntarily the quantum of saving without any outside pressure. It should however be ensured that the amount of savings should be such that the poorest or the weakest members of the group can contribute without stress. The other sources of capital of SHGs is amount provided by NGOs and others agencies, donations, interest realised on lending, interest on deposits, fine, recoveries and others. The distribution of study samples by capital resources is shown in the Table 4.8. (*See table on next page*)

Table 4.8 shows that savings is the major source of capital of the SHGs in all the districts of the study area. The second major source of capital is interest realised on lending and the other main source was from bank loan. The amount provided by the NGOs and other agencies stands in the fourth place. The capital collected from fine, interest on deposits and donations are in fifth, sixth and seventh place respectively in the area under study.

Investment

The common fund pooled by SHG members through savings, interest on deposits, donations etc., is invested in bank deposits, internal lending and other purposes. The investment of the SHGs in the area under study is depicted in the Table 4.9. (*See table on page 82*)

Table 4.9 depicts the distribution of study samples by investment of the SHGs. The SHGs in the study area invest the pooled amount on various heads such as bank deposit, internal lending, buildings and business. It is observed from the tables that, majority of the SHGs in the study area invest the pooled funds in internal lending.

Table 4.8: Distribution of Study Samples by Capital Resources

Districts	Savings		Amount Provided by NGO		Donation		Interest Realised on Lending		Interest on Deposits		Bank Loan		Fine	
	Nos	%	Nos	%	Nos	%	Nos	%	Nos	%	Nos	%	Nos	%
Bagalkot	97	97.00	23	23.00	3	3.00	88	88.00	10	10.00	71	71.00	12	12.00
Belgaum	126	99.21	21	16.54	8	6.30	105	82.68	8	6.30	76	59.84	14	11.02
Bijapur	145	96.67	37	24.67	3	2.00	136	90.67	10	6.67	117	78.00	18	12.00
Dharwad	115	97.46	29	24.58	8	6.78	99	83.90	13	11.02	76	64.41	9	7.63
Gadag	216	98.18	41	18.64	12	5.45	179	81.36	30	13.64	143	65.00	28	12.73
Haveri	77	95.06	18	22.22	3	3.70	69	85.19	4	4.94	53	65.43	9	11.11
Uttar Kannada	101	96.19	26	24.76	4	3.81	96	91.43	10	9.52	80	76.19	12	11.43
Total	**877**	**97.34**	**195**	**21.64**	**41**	**4.55**	**772**	**85.68**	**85**	**9.43**	**616**	**68.37**	**102**	**11.32**

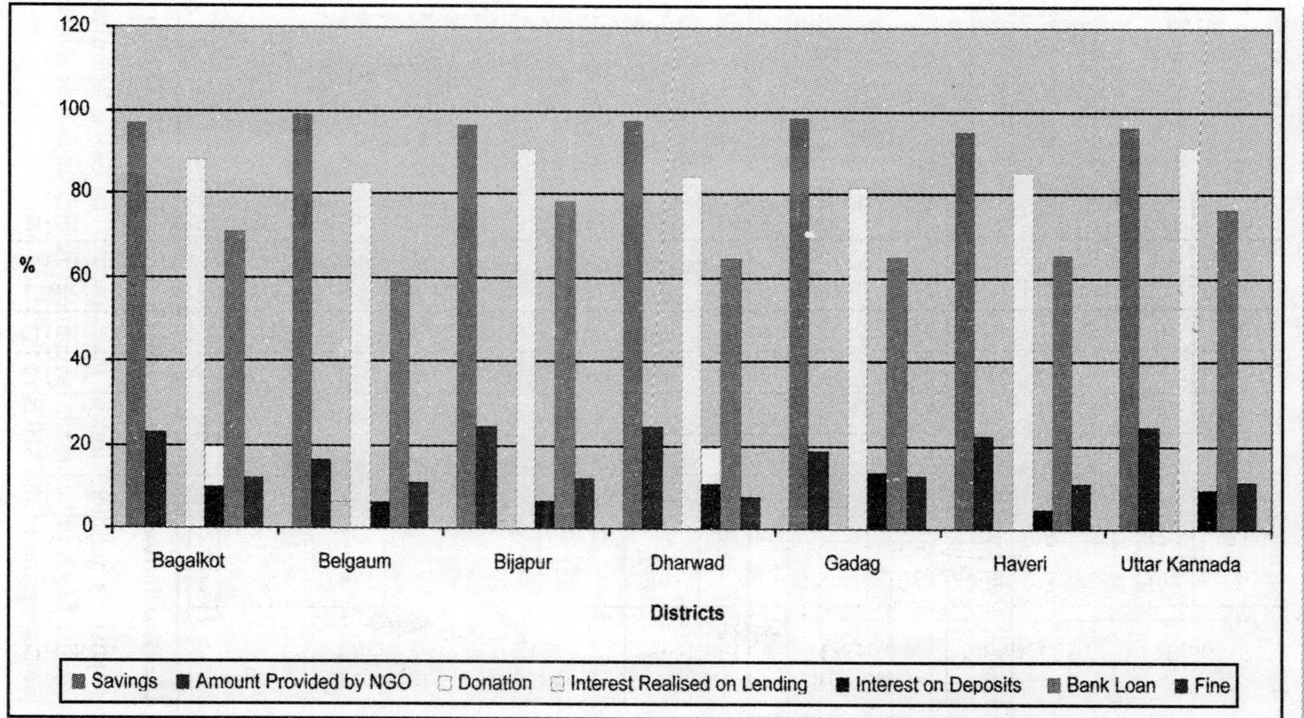

Fig. 4.2: Distribution of Study Samples by Capital Resources

Table 4.9: Distribution of Study Samples by Investment of the SHGs

Districts	Bank Deposit		Internal Lending		Building		Business	
	Nos	%	Nos	%	Nos	%	Nos	%
Bagalkot	35	35.00	56	56.00	2	2.00	12	12.00
Belgaum	62	48.82	70	55.12	0	0.00	14	11.02
Bijapur	42	28.00	82	54.67	2	1.33	18	12.00
Dharwad	60	50.85	60	50.85	1	0.85	9	7.63
Gadag	85	38.64	123	55.91	5	2.27	28	12.73
Haveri	38	46.91	33	40.74	1	1.23	9	11.11
Uttar Kannada	40	38.10	54	51.43	1	0.95	12	11.43
Total	**362**	**40.18**	**478**	**53.05**	**12**	**1.33**	**102**	**11.32**

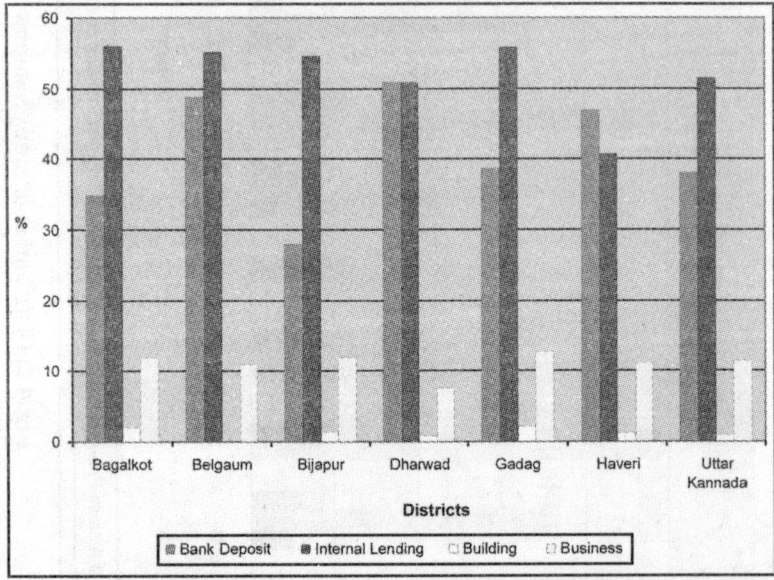

Fig. 4.3: Distribution of Study Samples by Investment of the SHGs

Bank deposit is another kind of investment. The SHGs are also investing the funds in business. Investment in buildings was found to be the last option of the SHGs in the study area.

Internal Lending

The mean savings of the SHGs and average own collection fund and mean loan from the banks is shown in the Table 4.10.

Table 4.10: Showing District-wise Average Savings and Internal Lending of SHGs

District	Mean Savings	Own Collection	Loan from Bank
Bagalkot	48306.08	55171.11	164963.64
Belgaum	52593.57	58021.37	204000.00
Bijapur	45481.47	53314.39	157802.08
Dharwad	55594.26	62656.19	190000.00
Gadag	51734.18	59196.91	183208.33
Haveri	51033.67	55952.05	179156.25
Uttar Kannada	51293.43	59375.51	164737.70
Total	**50832.47**	**57797.03**	**175565.50**

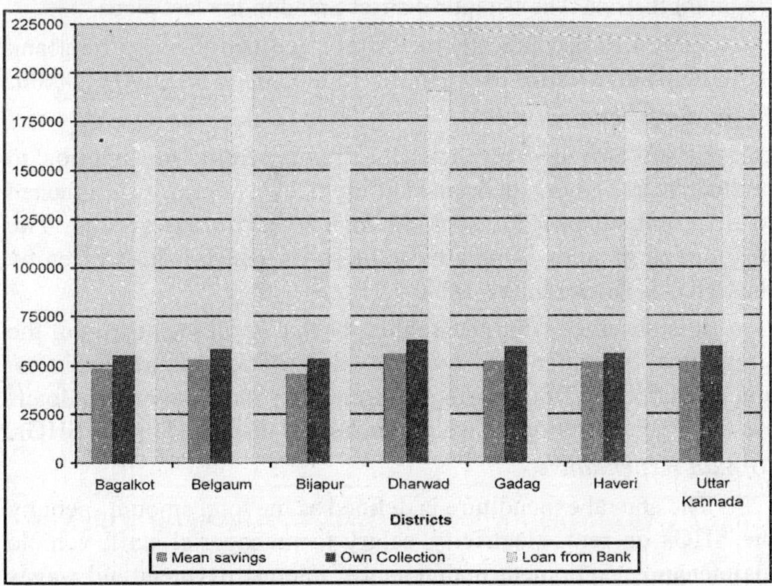

Fig. 4.4: Showing District-wise Average Saving and Internal Lending of SHGs

Table 4.10 indicates the district-wise average savings, collection and the loan obtained from the bank by the SHGs in the study area. The total average savings was Rs. 50832.47, own collection Rs. 57797.03 and loan form bank was Rs. 175565.50. With regards to savings, Dharwad district has the highest mean savings of Rs. 55594.26 and Bijapur district has the least *i.e.* Rs. 45487.47 savings. Belgaum and Gadag districts have means savings of Rs. 52593.57 and Rs. 51734.18 respectively. The mean savings of Uttar Kannada district was found to be Rs. 51293.13 followed by Haveri and Bagalkot districts with Rs. 57033.67, and Rs. 48306.08 respectively.

The internal lending of the SHGs in the study area constitutes two main components. One is own collection and another one component is loan from the bank. The loan obtained from the bank is a major component of internal lending in the study area. SHGs are also lending the amount to the member of the groups by own collection.

The average own collection ranges between Rs. 53314.49 to Rs. 62656.19. The Dharwad district has the lightest mean own collection followed by Uttar Kannada, Gadag, Belgaum, Haveri and Bagalkot district. The Bijapur district Stand in the last place.

Table 4.10 also indicates that the average loan obtained from bank in the study area varies between Rs. 157802.08 to Rs. 1,902,000.00.

Purpose of Loan

Loans provided by the SHG ranging from consumption to productive and emergent needs. Different level of priority is attached to different purpose of seeking loan by different groups. The distribution of study sample by purpose for which loan is given by the SHGs is shown in the Table 4.11.

It is observed from the Table 4.11 that in all the district of the study area the major loan was provided for agriculture, business, and education. Health, housing, consumption and repayment of loans are the others purpose for which the loan is disbursed by the SHGs.

Annual Expenditure

The annual expenditure is defined as the total amount spent by the SHGs on rent, electricity, salary to managerial staff, vehicle maintenance, equipment maintenance, interest payment and wages to workers etc. The annual expenditure of the SHGs is shown in the Table 4.12. (*See table on page 87*)

Table 4.11: Distribution of Study Samples by Purposes for which Loan is given by SHG

Districts	Agriculture		Education		Housing		Health		Business		Repayment of Loan		Consumption		Others	
	Nos	%	Nos	%	Nos	%	Nos	%	Nos	%	Nos	%	Nos	%	Nos	%
Bagalkot	59	59.00	15	15.00	11	11.00	8	8.00	70	70.00	3	3.00	8	8.00	4	4.00
Belgaum	90	70.87	17	13.39	10	7.87	7	5.51	59	46.46	14	11.02	11	8.66	0	0.00
Bijapur	73	48.67	17	11.33	13	8.67	11	7.33	116	77.33	3	2.00	12	8.00	4	2.67
Dharwad	77	65.25	23	19.49	16	13.56	8	6.78	78	66.10	8	6.78	14	11.86	3	2.54
Gadag	142	64.55	42	19.09	28	12.73	21	9.55	150	68.18	10	4.55	22	10.00	12	5.45
Haveri	56	69.14	11	13.58	7	8.64	4	4.94	44	54.32	5	6.17	4	4.94	0	0.00
Uttar Kannada	64	60.95	20	19.05	12	11.43	11	10.48	74	70.48	4	3.81	10	9.52	7	6.67
Total	**561**	**62.26**	**145**	**16.09**	**97**	**10.77**	**70**	**7.77**	**591**	**65.59**	**47**	**5.22**	**81**	**8.99**	**30**	**3.33**

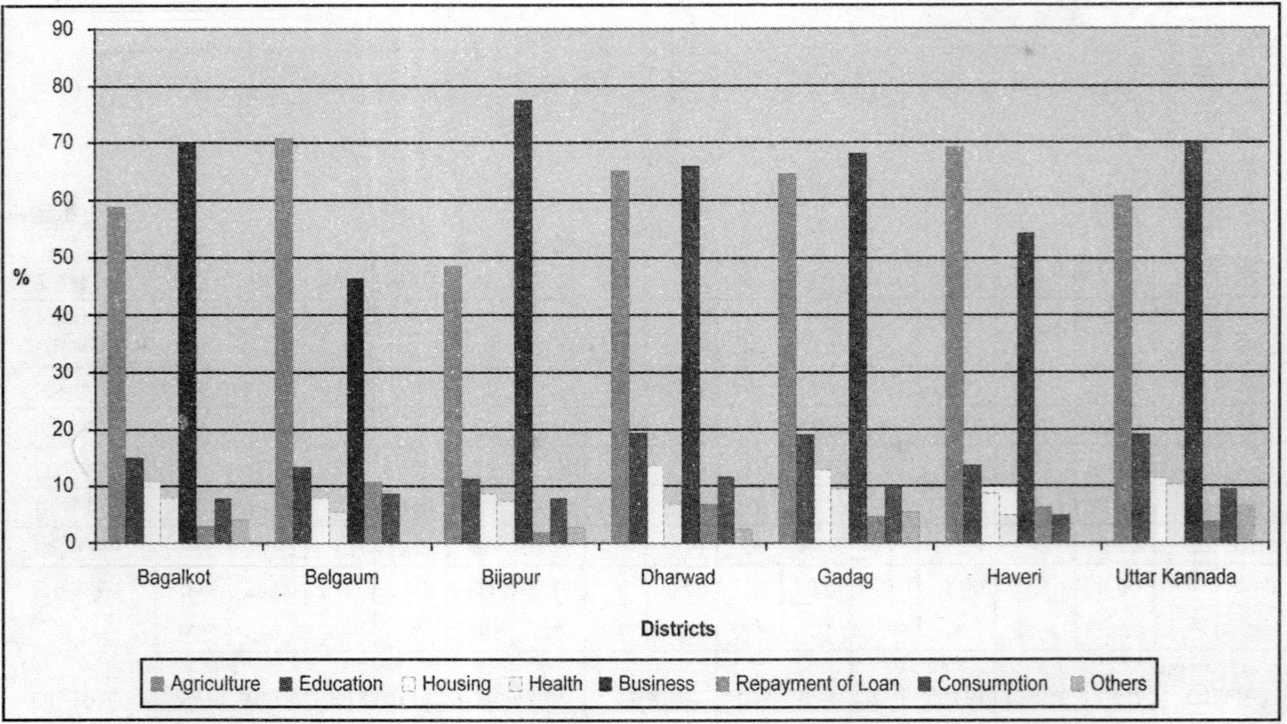

Fig. 4.5: Distribution of Study Samples by Purposes for which Loan is given by SHG

Table 4.12: Showing the Annual Expenditure of the SHGs

Districts	Rental		Salary of Management Staff		Electricity		Vehicle Maintenance		Building Maintenance		Equipment Maintenance		Interest Payment	
	Nos	%	Nos	%	Nos	%	Nos	%	Nos	%	Nos	%	Nos	%
Bagalkot	97	97.00	23	23.00	3	3.00	88	88.00	10	10.00	71	71.00	12	12.00
Belgaum	126	99.21	21	16.54	8	6.30	105	82.68	8	6.30	76	59.84	14	11.02
Bijapur	145	96.67	37	24.67	3	2.00	136	90.67	10	6.67	117	78.00	18	12.00
Dharwad	115	97.46	29	24.58	8	6.78	99	83.90	13	11.02	76	64.41	9	7.63
Gadag	216	98.18	41	18.64	12	5.45	179	81.36	30	13.64	143	65.00	28	12.73
Haveri	77	95.06	18	22.22	3	3.70	69	85.19	4	4.94	53	65.43	9	11.11
Uttar Kannada	101	96.19	26	24.76	4	3.81	96	91.43	10	9.52	80	76.19	12	11.43
Total	**877**	**97.34**	**195**	**21.64**	**41**	**4.55**	**772**	**85.68**	**85**	**9.43**	**616**	**68.37**	**102**	**11.32**

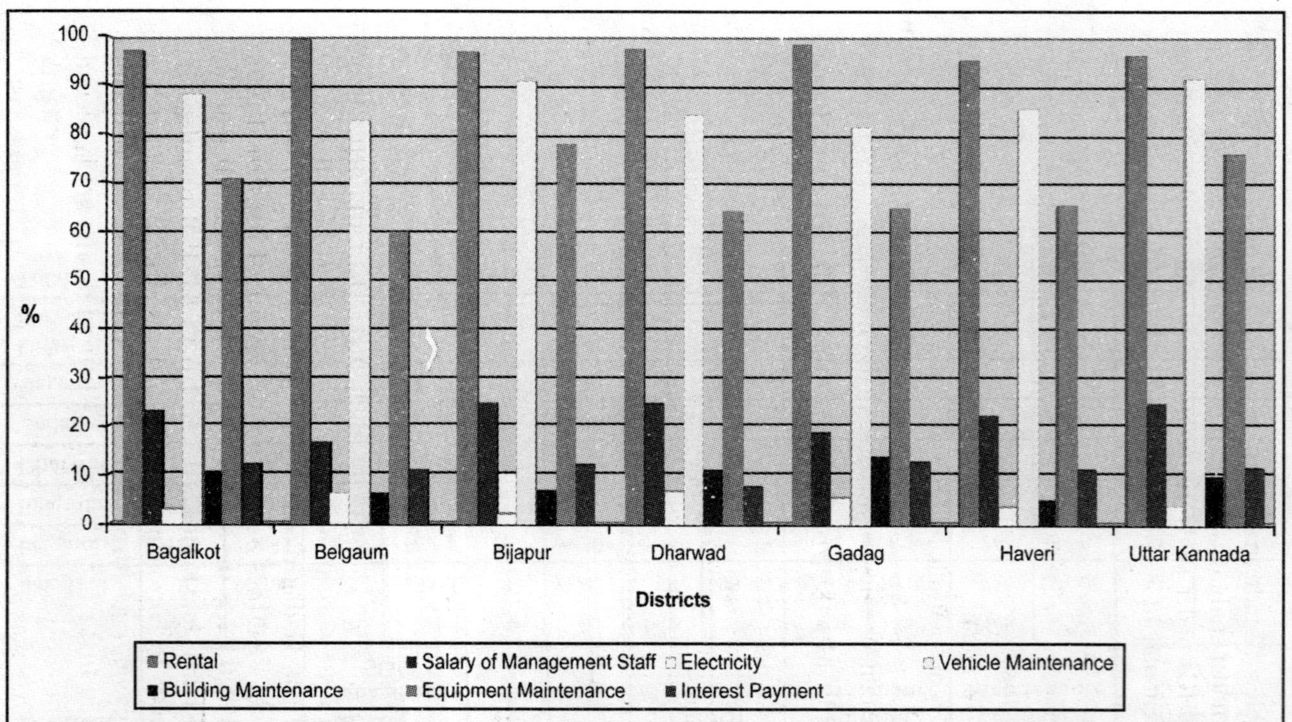

Fig. 4.6: Showing the Annual Expenditure of the SHGs

Table 4.12 indicates that the major expenditure of the SHGs of the area under study was found to be interest payment. Only 57 out of 901 SHGs under study are working in rental buildings and are paying rent and 72 SHGs are spending on electricity charges. This indicates that majority of the SHGs have no owned buildings and the SHGs are spending more on interest payment. The other heads of expenditure are insignificant in the area under study.

Deposits and Borrowings

Some amount of pooled fund is kept as deposit with the banks and SHGs are getting loans from the banks for lending to their members. The mean deposit and the mean borrowings of the SHGs in the area under study is indicated in the Table 4.13.

Table 4.13: Mean Deposits and Borrowings of the SHGs with Banks

District	Deposits (IX 2)	Barrowings (IX 3)
Bagalkot	45885.8	142182.8
Belgaum	53714.7	184395.0
Bijapur	41068.1	135127.7
Dharwad	48724.2	158952.4
Gadag	48123.8	168490.0
Haveri	45720.9	147684.2
UK	40749.8	124670.1
Total	**46976.4**	**153939.8**

Table 4.13 indicates the average deposits and borrowings of the SHGs with the banks in the study area. The mean deposits of Belgaum district was the highest with Rs. 53714.7 followed by Dharwad and Gadag district with Rs. 48724.2 and Rs. 48123.8 respectively. Rs. 45885.8 was the mean deposit of Bagalkot district and Rs. 45720.9 was the man deposit of Haveri district. Bijapur has Rs. 410681 and Uttar Kannada district has Rs. 40749.8 mean deposit. With regards to borrowing is concerned, the district wise average borrowings varying between Rs. 184395.5 to Rs. 124670.1. Belgaum district is in first place, Gadag and Dharwad district are in second and third place. Haveri, Bagalkot and Bijapur district are in fourth fifth and sixth place. The position of Uttar Kannada district is last.

Purpose-wise Borrowings

The SHGs of the study area are taking the loans from banks for various purposes. Agriculture, cottage and small enterprises, trade, dairying, consumption, meeting household expenses, health, repayment of old loans and others are the different purposes of getting loan by the SHGs. The purpose-wise borrowing by the SHGs from the banks is depicted in the Table 4.14.

Table 4.14 depicts the purpose-wise borrowings by the SHGs from the banks in all the districts of the study area. The banks are lending to the groups for various purposes such as agriculture, trade, small enterprises, dairy, consumption, housing health and repayment of loans. The major purposes of lending by the banks in the study area are trade and agriculture. The third purpose of lending was dairying. The other purposes for which loan is provided by the banks to the SHGs are not significant.

Actual Amount of Loan Requested by the SHGs from Banks

The banks in the study area are usually sanctioning the loan amount actually requested by the SHGs. The actual amount of loan requested by the SHGs from the banks and mean per cent of loan obtained in relation to the amount applied far is shown in the Table 4.15 and 4.16. (*See tables on page 93*)

The actual amount of loan requested by the SHGs from the bank in the study area is shown in the Table 4.15. It is reflected from the table that, 65.59 per cent of the study sample said yes and the remaining 34.41 per cent gave negative response. Through the district-wise percentage varies, but the majority groups said that the banks are providing loan to the extent requested by the SHGs in the study area. The Chi-Square value is 8.4683 and Pearson's R is 0.2064 showing no significant relationship between actual amount of loan requested and the actual amount of loan given by the banks in the study area.

Mean Per cent of Loan Obtained

Table 4.16 depicts the district-wise average per cent of loan obtained in relation to the amount applied. The mean per cent of Haveri district was highest with 71.32 followed by Uttar Kannada and Bagalkot districts with 71.32 and 69.86 respectively.

Table 4.14: Distribution of Study Samples by Purpose-wise Borrowings by the SHGs from Banks

Districts	Agriculture		Cottage and SSI		Trade		Dairying		Consumption		Household Employment		Health		Repayment of Old Loan	
	Nos	%	Nos	%	Nos	%	Nos	%	Nos	%	Nos	%	Nos	%	Nos	%
Bagalkot	44	44.00	5	5.00	83	83.00	14	14.00	7	7.00	4	4.00	5	5.00	1	1.00
Belgaun	77	60.63	0	0.00	68	53.54	13	10.24	1	0.79	1	0.79	1	0.79	1	0.79
Bijapur	53	35.33	7	4.67	133	88.67	20	13.33	11	7.33	4	2.67	8	5.33	1	0.67
Dharwad	57	48.31	2	1.69	82	69.49	18	15.25	8	6.78	6	5.08	5	4.24	3	2.54
Gadag	116	52.73	13	5.91	174	79.09	45	20.45	19	8.64	16	7.27	14	6.36	4	1.82
Haveri	43	53.09	3	3.70	56	69.14	14	17.28	3	3.70	1	1.23	3	3.70	1	1.23
Uttar Kannada	49	46.67	7	6.67	88	83.81	20	19.05	9	8.57	6	5.71	5	4.76	0	0.00
Total	**439**	**48.72**	**37**	**4.11**	**684**	**75.92**	**144**	**15.98**	**58**	**6.44**	**38**	**4.22**	**41**	**4.55**	**11**	**1.22**

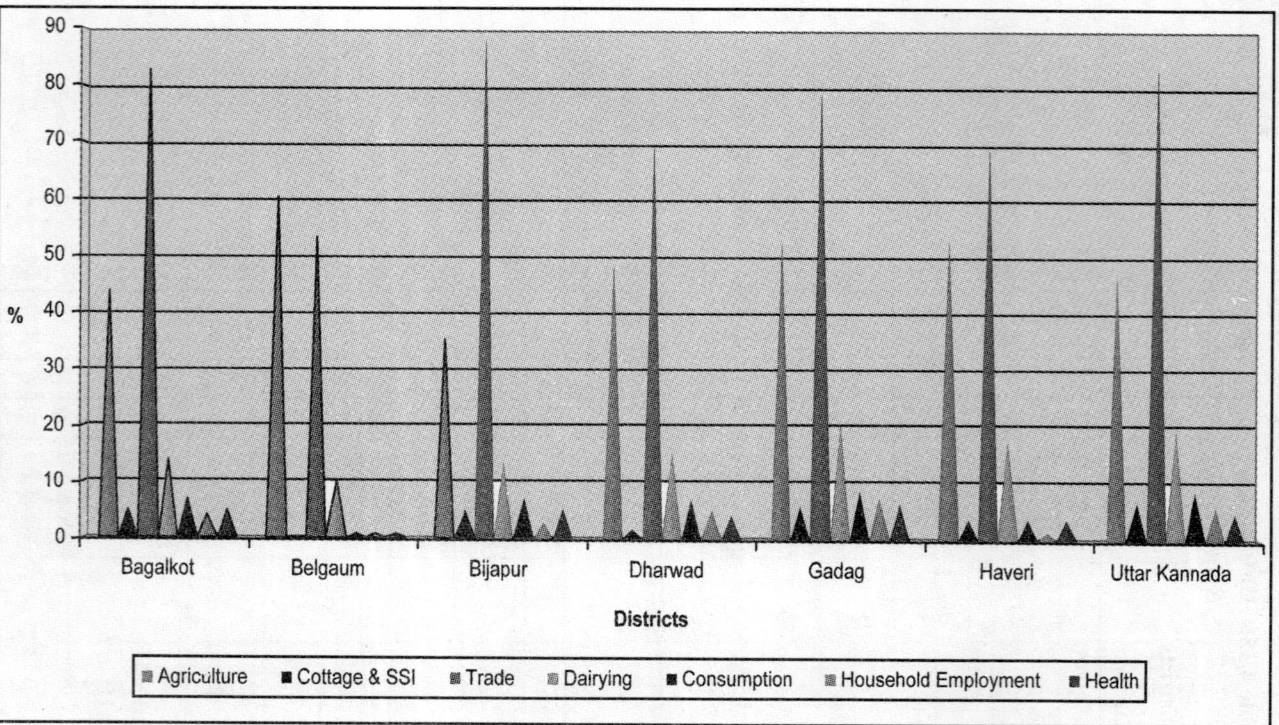

Fig. 4.7: Distribution of Study Samples by Purpose-wise Borrowing by the SHGs from Banks

Table 4.15: Distribution of Study Samples by Actual Amount of Loan Requested by the SHGs from Banks

Districts	Yes	%	No	%	Total	%
Bagalkot	64	64.00	36	36.00	100	11.10
Belgaum	91	71.65	36	28.35	127	14.10
Bijapur	104	69.33	46	30.67	150	16.65
Dharwad	82	69.49	36	30.51	118	13.10
Gadag	138	62.73	82	37.27	220	24.42
Haveri	45	55.56	36	44.44	81	8.99
Uttar Kannada	67	63.81	38	36.19	105	11.65
Total	**591**	**65.59**	**310**	**34.41**	**901**	**100.00**

Chi-square = 8.4683, P = 0.2064, NS

Table 4.16: Mean Per cent of Loan Obtained in Relation to the Amount Applied

Districts	Mean Per cent of Loan Obtained in Relation to the Amount
Bagalkot	69.86
Belgaum	66.11
Bijapur	69.24
Dharwad	67.64
Gadag	67.38
Haveri	71.39
Uttar Kannada	71.32
Total	**68.77**

The average per cent of loan obtained in relation to the amount applied of Bijapur, Dharwad, Gadag and Belgaum districts was found to be 69.24, 67.64, 67.38 and 66.11 respectively.

Banks Fixing-up Maximum Limit of Loan to SHGs for Different Purposes

Banks under study are following their own policies in issuing loans. They also have to follow HO guidelines, RBI rules, and

NABARD guidelines. Some banks fix-up maximum limit of loan for different purposes and some are not. The banks fixing the maximum limit of loan to SHG for different purposes in the study area is shown in the Table 4.17.

Table 4.17: Banks Fixing-up Maximum Limit of Loan to SHGs for Different Purposes

Districts	Yes	%	No	%	Total	%
Bagalkot	64	64.00	36	36.00	100	11.10
Belgaum	91	71.65	36	28.35	127	14.10
Bijapur	104	69.33	46	30.67	150	16.65
Dharwad	82	69.49	36	30.51	118	13.10
Gadag	138	62.73	82	37.27	220	24.42
Haveri	45	55.56	36	44.44	81	8.99
Uttar Kannada	67	63.81	38	36.19	105	11.65
Total	**591**	**65.59**	**310**	**34.41**	**901**	**100.00**
Chi-square = 8.4683, P = 0.2063, NS						

It is indicated by the tables that, majority of the banks are not fixing the maximum limit of loan to SHGs for different purposes. This indicates that the banks in the study area are fixing the limit on the basis of the amount needed by groups and requirements for the completion of the project. The Chi-Square value in this case is 8.4683 and Pearson's R is 0.2063. Hence, there is no relationship between purpose of loan and fixing maximum limit.

Adequacy of Bank Loan

Banks in the study area, while issuing loans, looks into the purpose for which the loan is demanded and also obtains the project details of the SHGs investment. The banks usually pay loans which are needed by the SHGs. The adequacy of bank loan to SHGs is indicated in the Table 4.18.

Majority of the study groups gave positive response. 65.59 per cent groups said yes and the remaining 34.41 per cent of the SHGs gave negative response with regards to adequacy of bank loans.

Table 4.18: Distribution of Study Samples by Adequacy of Bank Loan to SHGs

Districts	Yes	%	No	%	Total	%
Bagalkot	64	64.00	36	36.00	100	11.10
Belgaum	91	71.65	36	28.35	127	14.10
Bijapur	104	69.33	46	30.67	150	16.65
Dharwad	82	69.49	36	30.51	118	13.10
Gadag	138	62.73	82	37.27	220	24.42
Haveri	45	55.56	36	44.44	81	8.99
Uttar Kannada	67	63.81	38	36.19	105	11.65
Total	**591**	**65.59**	**310**	**34.41**	**901**	**100.00**

Additional Loan

SHGs can get loans from the banks any number of times but, the provision of additional loan can be availed before the earlier loan is repaid depends on repayment capacity, encashment feasibility, etc. The provision of the bank additional loan to SHGs before the earlier loan is repaid in the study area is shown in Table 4.19

Table 4.19: Provision of Bank Additional Loan/Working Capital to SHGs before the Earlier Loan is Repaid

Districts	Yes	%	No	%	Total	%
Bagalkot	64	64.00	36	36.00	100	11.10
Belgaum	91	71.65	36	28.35	127	14.10
Bijapur	104	69.33	46	30.67	150	16.65
Dharwad	82	69.49	36	30.51	118	13.10
Gadag	138	62.73	82	37.27	220	24.42
Haveri	45	55.56	36	44.44	81	8.99
Uttar Kannada	67	63.81	38	36.19	105	11.65
Total	**591**	**65.59**	**310**	**34.41**	**901**	**100.00**

Chi-square = 8.4683, P = 0.2063, NS

Table 4.19 clearly indicates that the majority of the banks in the study area are providing additional loan or working capital before the earlier loan is repaid. The percentage of positive response from SHGs in the study area was found to be 65.59 and the percentage of negative response was 34.41. The Chi-Square value is 8.4683 and Pearson's R is 0.2063. Therefore, provision of additional loans to SHGs before the earlier loan is repaid is not significant in the study area.

Nature of Security

The SHGs are keeping various types of securities while getting loans from the banks. Buildings, deposits and guarantee from the NGOs are the types of securities the banks insist in providing loans to SHGs. Table 4.20 indicates the type of security insisted by the banks in the study area in providing loans to SHGs.

Table 4.20: Types of Securities Bank Insist in Providing Loans to SHGs

Districts	Buildings	%	Deposits	%	Guarantees	%
Bagalkot	15	15.00	15	15.00	93	93.00
Belgaum	14	11.02	20	15.75	120	94.49
Bijapur	37	24.67	28	18.67	139	92.67
Dharwad	14	11.86	24	20.34	108	91.53
Gadag	28	12.73	34	15.45	200	90.91
Haveri	10	12.35	8	9.88	77	95.06
Uttar Kannada	22	20.95	21	20.00	89	84.76
Total	**140**	**15.54**	**150**	**16.65**	**826**	**91.68**
Chi-square = 16.8845, P = 0.1540, NS						

Various types of securities such as buildings, deposits, guarantees of NGOs, etc., are demanded by the banks in the study area. Majority of the banks insist guarantees of NGO followed by deposits and buildings as collateral securities. In all the district of the study area, same priorities accorded while providing loan to the SHGs. The Chi-Square value is 16.8845 and Pearson's R is 0.1540 showing no significant relationship between security insisted by the banks in the study area and provision of loans.

Usual Time-taken by the Banks in Releasing Loans to SHGs

Banks under study require some days of time for the scrutiny of the application of the SHGs seeking loan. The usual time taken by the banks in releasing the loans to SHGs of the study area is depicted in the Table 4.21.

Table 4.21: Usual Time-taken by the Banks in Releasing Loans to SHGs

Districts	Mean Time in Days
Bagalkot	2.88
Belgaum	2.60
Bijapur	2.82
Dharwad	3.51
Gadag	3.36
Haveri	3.26
Uttar Kannada	2.45
Total	**3.01**

The mean time in days taken by the banks in releasing the loans to SHGs was registered 3.01 days. Uttar Kannada district has 2.45 mean time days and Belgaum has 2.60 mean time days. The mean time days of Bijapur, Bagalkot and Haveri district are 2.82, 2.88 and 3.26 respectively. Mean time days taken by the banks in case of Gadag and Dharwad districts were found to be 3.36 and 3.51.

Procedure of Obtaining Loans from Banks

The SHGs, while obtaining loan from the banks have to follow certain procedure and have to submit some documents. The opinions' relating to bank procedure were collected under four heads such as: *(i)* simple, *(ii)* time consuming, *(iii)* cumbersome and *(iv)* involves more paper work. The procedure of obtaining loans from banks in the study area is shown in the Table 4.22. (*See table on next page*)

Table 4.22 shows the procedure of obtaining loans from banks in the study area. Majority of the groups are of the opinion that the procedure is simple and not cumbersome. 90.68 per cent of the groups agreed that the bank procedure is simple, 5.55 per cent groups said that the procedure is time consuming and 2.33 per cent and 1.44 per cent of the groups expressed that the loan procedure involved more paper work and cumbersome in the study area.

Table 4.22: Procedure of Obtaining Loans from Banks

Districts	Simple	%	Time Consu-ming	%	Cumber-some	%	More Paper Work	%
Bagalkot	90	90.00	06	6.00	1	1.00	3	3.00
Belgaum	117	92.13	05	3.94	3	2.36	2	1.57
Bijapur	139	92.67	07	4.67	1	0.67	3	2.00
Dharwad	110	93.22	04	3.39	1	0.85	3	2.54
Gadag	200	90.90	09	4.09	4	1.82	7	3.18
Haveri	67	82.71	10	12.35	2	2.47	2	2.47
Uttar Kannada	94	89.52	09	8.57	1	0.95	1	0.95
Total	**817**	**90.68**	**50**	**5.55**	**13**	**1.44**	**21**	**2.33**
Chi-square = 36.2773, P = 0.0065, S								

It is observed from the Table 4.22 that the Chi-Square value in this case is 36.2773 and the Pearson's R is 0.0065 indicating a significant relationship between loan procedure and loans obtained.

Interest Subsidy

The government pays subsidy to some schemes or programmes. SGSY is a government programme with subsidy and SHG bank linkage is a non subsidy programme. Getting interest subsidy by the SHGs in the study area and prompt receipt of the subsidy amount is depicted in the Tables 4.23 and 4.24.

Table 4.23: Getting Interest Subsidy by the SHGs

Districts	Yes	%	No	%	Total	%
Bagalkot	14	14.00	86	86.00	100	11.10
Belgaum	11	8.66	116	91.34	127	14.10
Bijapur	20	13.33	130	86.67	150	16.65
Dharwad	20	16.95	98	83.05	118	13.10
Gadag	35	15.91	185	84.09	220	24.42
Haveri	8	9.88	73	90.12	81	8.99
Uttar Kannada	11	10.48	94	89.52	105	11.65
Total	**119**	**13.21**	**782**	**86.79**	**901**	**100.00**

The interest subsidy taken by the SHGs in the study area is depicted in the Table 4.23. It is observed from Table 4.23 that, 86.79 per cent of SHGs do not get interest subsidy from the government or from any other agencies, only 13.21 SHG groups are getting interest subsidy in the area under study.

Receipt of Subsidy Amount

Table 4.24 indicates the district-wise prompt receipt of subsidy amount by the SHGs of the study area. Majority of respondents from all the districts gave negative response and only a small section of the respondents gave positive opinion. This depicts that the respondents do not receive the subsidy amount promptly.

Table 4.24: Prompt Receipt of Subsidy Amount by SHGs

Districts	Yes	%	No	%	Total	%
Bagalkot	4	4.00	96	96.00	100	11.10
Belgaum	2	1.57	125	98.43	127	14.10
Bijapur	6	4.00	144	96.00	150	16.65
Dharwad	6	5.08	112	94.92	118	13.10
Gadag	12	5.45	208	94.55	220	24.42
Haveri	3	3.70	78	96.30	81	8.99
Uttar Kannada	3	2.86	102	97.14	105	11.65
Total	**36**	**4.00**	**865**	**96.00**	**901**	**100.00**

Passing of Subsidy Benefits

The SHGS after receiving the subsidy amount will have to pass the same to their members. The passing of subsidy benefits to member borrowers is shown in the Table 4.25. (*See table on next page*)

It is observed from Table 4.25 that 90.12 per cent of the respondents expressed negative response and the remaining 9.88 per cent respondents gave positive response. This shows that in all the districts, subsidy benefits are not passed to the member borrowers promptly.

Utilisation and Impact of Bank Loan

The SHGs are obtaining the loans from banks for various purposes. The obtained loan should be used properly, and then only the poor members will come out from the clutches of poverty.

Table 4.25: Passing of Subsidy Benefits to Member Borrower

Districts	Yes	%	No	%	Total	%
Bagalkot	13	13.00	87	87.00	100	11.10
Belgaum	2	1.57	125	98.43	127	14.10
Bijapur	21	14.00	129	86.00	150	16.65
Dharwad	12	10.17	106	89.83	118	13.10
Gadag	25	11.36	195	88.64	220	24.42
Haveri	5	6.17	76	93.83	81	8.99
Uttar Kannada	11	10.48	94	89.52	105	11.65
Total	**89**	**9.88**	**812**	**90.12**	**901**	**100.00**

The utilisation of loan obtained from the bank is depicted in the Tables 4.26.

Table 4.26: Utilisation of Loan Obtained from Banks

Districts	Yes	%	No	%	Total	%
Bagalkot	82	82.00	18	18.00	100	11.10
Belgaum	62	48.82	65	51.18	127	14.10
Bijapur	132	88.00	18	12.00	150	16.65
Dharwad	82	69.49	36	30.51	118	13.10
Gadag	152	69.09	68	30.91	220	24.42
Haveri	55	67.90	26	32.10	81	8.99
Uttar Kannada	90	85.71	15	14.29	105	11.65
Total	**655**	**72.70**	**246**	**27.30**	**901**	**100.00**
Chi-square = 70.4915 P = 0.0000, S						

The distribution of study samples by utilisation of loan from banks in the study area is highlighted in Table 4.26. Major partition of the respondents agreed that they are fully utilising the loan amount obtained from the banks. Only 27.30 per cent of the respondents disagree with regards to the utilisation. In case of, Belgaum district of the study area. About 51.18 per cent of the respondent groups expressed that they are not utilising the amount properly and the remaining 48.82 per cent groups said that they are utilising the loan amount properly. The Chi-Square value is 70.4915 and Pearson's R is 0.0000 showing a significant relationship between loan obtained from the banks and utilisation.

Type of Members of SHGs Availed Loan

The type of member implies that whether they are BPL members or APL members. Table 4.27 depicts the details of the type of members of the SHG who have availed loan in the study area.

Table 4.27: Details of the type of Members of SHGs Availed Loan

Districts	Mean Members-BPL	Mean Members-APL
Bagalkot	10.06	7.71
Belgaum	9.50	11.54
Bijapur	10.33	6.95
Dharwad	9.75	9.79
Gadag	10.41	8.89
Haveri	9.56	8.58
Uttar Kannada	10.32	7.37
Total	**10.07**	**8.85**

Table 4.27 indicates that the mean BPL members of the SHG who have availed loan are registered 10.07 per cent and APL members registered at 8.85 per cent. In all the districts of the study area the mean BPL members of the group who have availed loan was more pronounced than APL members. Hence it is come to a conclusion that BPL members are more benefiting by availing loans and SHGs are trying hard in supplying the credit to the poorer section of the area under study.

Number of Times Loan Availed

Poverty cannot be eradicated with a single loan. The micro-credit scheme seeks to promote multiple credit rather than one time credit. The distribution of study samples by number of times the loan is availed by the members of the SHGs and mean number of members taken repeated finance in the study area is shown in the Table 4.28 and Table 4.29.

Table 4.28: Number of Times Loan Availed by Members of the SHGs

Districts	1 Time	%	2 Time	%	3 Time	%	>3 Time	%
Bagalkot	62	62.00	42	42.00	19	19.00	17	17.00
Belgaum	117	92.13	47	37.01	41	32.28	44	34.65
Bijapur	80	53.33	68	45.33	25	16.67	23	15.33
Dharwad	91	77.12	48	40.68	25	21.19	25	21.19
Gadag	146	66.36	106	48.18	54	24.55	58	26.36
Haveri	64	79.01	27	33.33	13	16.05	14	17.28
Uttar Kannada	61	58.10	43	40.95	20	19.05	18	17.14
Total	**621**	**68.92**	**381**	**42.29**	**197**	**21.86**	**199**	**22.09**

It is observed from Table 4.28 that 68.92 per cent of the members of the SHGs availed loan for the first time and 42.29 per cent member availed loan twice, 21.86 per cent members have taken loan thrice and 22.09 per cent obtained loan repeatedly. This indicates that majority of the groups in the study area are new. Hence, they have taken single loan.

Repeat Finance

Table 4.29 indicates the mean number of members taken repeat finance in the study area. The mean number of members taken repeat loan was found to be 13.33. Belgaum district registered the highest with 14.07 mean numbers of members taken repeat loan and the

Table 4.29: Number of Members Taken Repeat Finance

Districts	Mean Number of me
Bagalkot	13.17
Belgaum	14.07
Bijapur	12.60
Dharwad	13.57
Gadag	13.41
Haveri	13.65
Uttar Kannada	12.26
Total	**13.33**

Uttar Kannada district is in last position with 12.26. The mean numbers of members taken repeat loan in Haveri, Dharwad, Gadag, Bagalkot and Bijapur districts-was 13.65, 13.57, 13.41, 13.17 and 12.60 respectively.

Impact of Bank Loan on Members

Bank loan has made a positive impact on the members of the groups. Their income and assets have gone up, improvement in the infrastructure, agriculture, dairying, better education; health of their children and in total living standard has been raised. Table 4.30 shows the economic impact of bank loan on the members of the SHGs in the study area.

The bank loan has made a positive impact on the members of the SHGs in all the district of the study area. Their investment in fixed asset has gone up and there is an improvement in the infrastructure *viz*., lighting, storage, transport of members, etc. Their dependence on money lenders has come down and the members have benefited in education of their children, health expenses, marriage expenditure etc. Loans have helped the members in the improvement of the agriculture and in meeting marketing expenses. The overall income of the members in the study area has gone up, dairying improved and totally the living standard has been raised.

It is observed from the Table 4.30 that 94.12 per cent member groups expressed that the living standard has gone up and 89.23 per cent SHGs responded that loans have helped in meeting the marketing operations. The percentage of improvement of agriculture of members was found to be 88.46, the percentage of members have benefited in education, health and others was 85.24, overall improvement in income of the members registered at 82.46 per cent and 68.04 per cent expressed that their dependence on money lenders has been reduced and the percentage of improvement in dairying was 62.38. The percentage of improvement in infrastructure was found to be 58.83 and the percentage of improvement in working capital was 52.83. Only 48.28 per cent respond that their investment in fixed assets has gone up.

Table 4.30: Impact of Bank Loan on Members

Districts	1		2		3		4		5	
	Nos	%	Nos	%	Nos	%	Nos	%	Nos	%
Bagalkot	50	50.00	62	62.00	57	57.00	73	73.00	82	82.00
Belgaum	41	32.28	52	40.94	43	33.86	67	52.76	107	84.25
Bijapur	94	62.67	106	70.67	97	64.67	119	79.33	131	87.33
Dharwad	52	44.07	66	55.93	61	51.69	75	63.56	101	85.59
Gadag	107	48.64	135	61.36	125	56.82	154	70.00	200	90.91
Haveri	32	39.51	40	49.38	34	41.98	46	56.79	63	77.78
Uttar Kannada	59	56.19	69	65.71	59	56.19	79	75.24	84	80.00
Total	**435**	**48.28**	**530**	**58.82**	**476**	**52.83**	**613**	**68.04**	**768**	**85.24**

Contd...

Districts	6		7		8		9		10	
	Nos	%	Nos	%	Nos	%	Nos	%	Nos	%
Bagalkot	84	84.00	82	82.00	57	57.00	76	76.00	94	94.00
Belgaum	116	91.34	121	95.28	85	66.93	110	86.61	117	92.13
Bijapur	134	89.33	129	86.00	90	60.00	124	82.67	144	96.00
Dharwad	107	90.68	105	88.98	80	67.80	102	86.44	111	94.07
Gadag	206	93.64	203	92.27	147	66.82	187	85.00	214	97.27
Haveri	68	83.95	68	83.95	42	51.85	63	77.78	71	87.65
Uttar Kannada	89	84.76	89	84.76	61	58.10	81	77.14	97	92.38
Total	804	89.23	797	88.46	562	62.38	743	82.46	848	94.12

Note: 1 = Investment in Fixed Assets; 2 = Investment in Infrastructure; 3 = Working Capital Position Improved; 4 = Less Dependence on Money Lenders; 5 = Education Benefits; 6 = Marketing Operations; 7 = Improvement in Agriculture; 8 = Improvement in Dairying; 9 = Overall Income Gone up; 10 = Standard of Living Increased.

Table 4.31: Installments of Loans Fixed by the SHGs

Districts	Farm Loan		SSI		Cottage Industry		Small Trade		Dairying		Food Industry		Others	
	Nos	%	Nos	%	Nos	%	Nos	%	Nos	%	Nos	%	Nos	%
Bagalkot	62	62.00	28	28.00	27	27.00	63	63.00	32	32.00	25	25.00	24	24.00
Belgaum	86	67.72	10	7.87	10	7.87	52	40.94	13	10.24	10	7.87	9	7.09
Bijapur	98	65.33	61	40.67	62	41.33	110	73.33	65	43.33	58	38.67	57	38.00
Dharwad	74	62.71	22	18.64	21	17.80	67	56.78	31	26.27	21	17.80	17	14.41
Gadag	138	62.73	53	24.09	48	21.82	143	65.00	72	32.73	44	20.00	32	14.55
Haveri	55	67.90	13	16.05	15	18.52	43	53.09	16	19.75	13	16.05	12	14.81
Uttar Kannada	63	60.00	29	27.62	31	29.52	61	58.10	30	28.57	28	26.67	29	27.62
Total	**576**	**63.93**	**216**	**23.97**	**214**	**23.75**	**539**	**59.82**	**259**	**28.75**	**199**	**22.09**	**180**	**19.98**

Chi-square = 90.3878, P = 0.0000, S

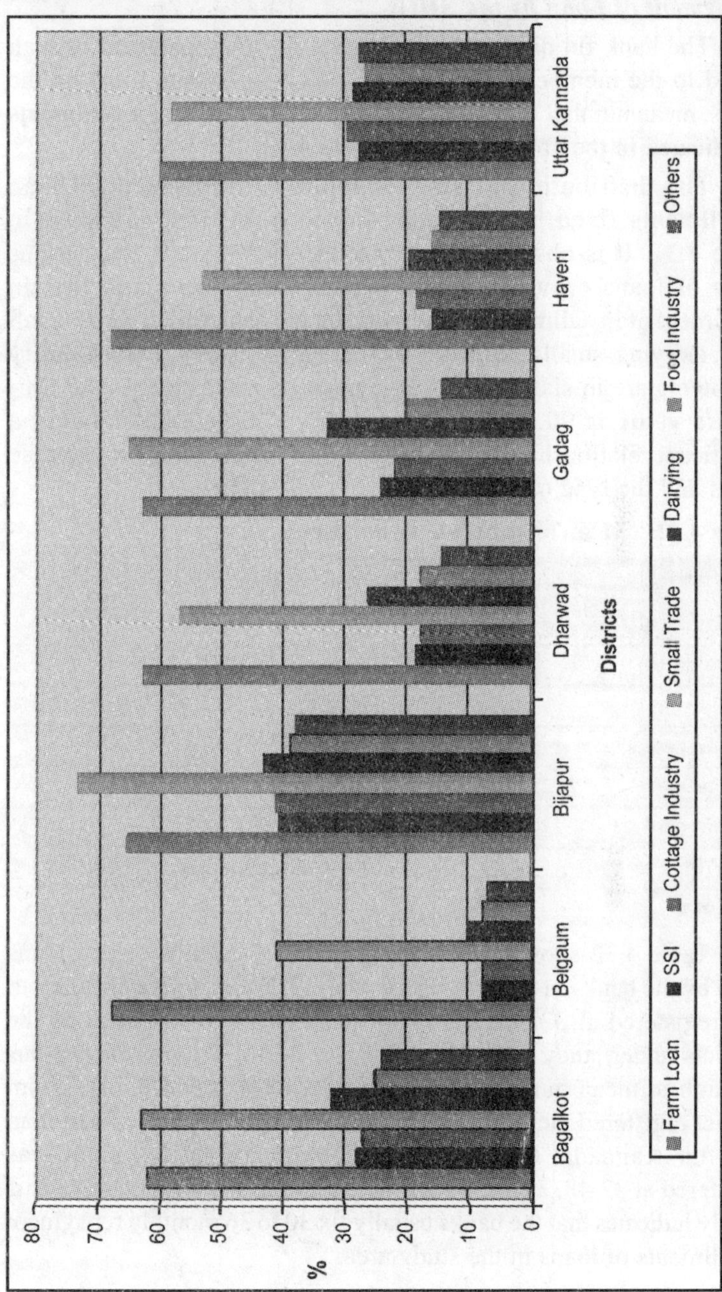

Fig. 4.8: Installments of Loans Fixed by the SHGs

Repayment of Loan by the SHGs

The bank fix different installments for the repayment of loan issued to the members. The type of loan installments fixed by the banks, mean number of installments and convenience of installments is indicated in the Tables 4.31, 4.32 and 4.33.

The distribution of study samples by repayment of loan installments fixed by the banks in the study area is shown in Table 4.31. It is observed from the table that among the various types of loans provided by the banks, farm loan stand first in repayment of installment of loan fixed by the bank followed by small trade, dairying, small enterprises and cottage industries. Food industry and others are in sixth and seventh position respectively. The Chi-Square value is 90.3878 and Pearson's R is 0.0000 showing a significant relationship between number of installments fixed by the banks and the type of loans.

Table 4.32: Mean Numbers of Installments

Districts	Mean Number of Installments
Bagalkot	31.70
Belgaum	30.85
Bijapur	34.15
Dharwad	31.51
Gadag	31.72
Haveri	31.22
Uttar Kannada	32.48
Total	**32.02**

Table 4.32 shows the mean numbers of installments of loans fixed by the banks in the area under study. The total mean installment was registered at 32.02. The mean installments of the loan of the districts under study vary from 30.85 to 34.15. Bijapur district has the highest mean number of installments of loan and the Belgaum district registered the least. The mean number of installments of loan of Uttar Kannada, Gadag, Haveri, Dharwad and Bagalkot was registered at 32.48, 31.72, 31.22, 31.51 and 31.70 respectively. This clearly indicates that the banks usually fix 30 to 36 monthly repayment installments of loans in the study area.

Convenience in Installments

The convenience of the loan repayment installments of the study area is shown in the Table 4.33. Majority of the respondents of the district under study agree that the loan repayment installments are convenient. The percentage of the convenience of the loan repayment installment was found to be 93.45 and 6.55 per cent disagree that the installments are convenient. This shows that the members are comfortable and they do not have any force or pressure in the repayment of loan in the study area.

Table 4.33: Distribution of Study Samples by Convenience in Installments

Districts	Yes	%	No	%	Total	%
Bagalkot	92	92.00	8	8.00	100	11.10
Belgaum	122	96.06	5	3.94	127	14.10
Bijapur	143	95.33	7	4.67	150	16.65
Dharwad	109	92.37	9	7.63	118	13.10
Gadag	208	94.55	12	5.45	220	24.42
Haveri	71	87.65	10	12.35	81	8.99
Uttar Kannada	97	92.38	8	7.62	105	11.65
Total	**842**	**93.45**	**59**	**6.55**	**901**	**100.00**

Relief from the Banks on Request

Some of the SHGs of the study area are getting relief from banks on request with regards to repayment of loans. Getting relief from the banks with regard to loan installments and inconveniences of loan installments are depicted in the Table 4.34 and Table 4.35. (*See tables on next page*)

Table 4.34 shows that getting relief from banks for inconveniences of loan installments in the study area. Table 4.34 indicates that 68.15 per cent of SHGs do not get any relief from the banks on request for inconveniences of loan installment. Only 31.85 per cent SHGs gets relief from the banks. This clearly indicates that the banks in the study area are strictly adhering to their policies.

Table 4.34: Getting Relief from the Banks on Request

Districts	Yes	%	No	%	Total	%
Bagalkot	37	37.00	63	63.00	100	11.10
Belgaum	23	18.11	104	81.89	127	14.10
Bijapur	67	44.67	83	55.33	150	16.65
Dharwad	32	27.12	86	72.88	118	13.10
Gadag	70	31.82	150	68.18	220	24.42
Haveri	21	25.93	60	74.07	81	8.99
Uttar Kannada	37	35.24	68	64.76	105	11.65
Total	**287**	**31.85**	**614**	**68.15**	**901**	**100.00**

Types of Inconveniences

The district-wise types of inconveniences of the loan installments in the study area are depicted in the Table 4.35. The respondents under study agree that the installments of loan are limited and the amount is heavy, interest cost is more, bank policies are rigid and the banks are levying heavy penalty for late payment. The other inconveniences are; subsidy not released in time, income of the SHG is not growing fast, etc. (*See table on next page*)

Table 4.35 indicates that the major inconveniences of the SHGs with regard to loan installments are more interest cost, member are not prompt and hence SHG finds it difficult to keep up the schedule, income of the SHG is not growing fast, subsidy not released in time and rigid bank policies. The other causes are insignificant. The Chi-Square value is 115.2459 and Pearson's R is 0.0000 showing a significant relationship between type of inconveniences and repayment of loans.

TABLES RELATING TO BANKS

Numbers of Employees in the Bank

The number of employees in the bank differs from bank to bank and branch to branch. The average employees in the banks under study are shown in the Table 4.36. (*See table on page 113*)

Table 4.35: Distribution of Study Samples by Types of Inconveniences

Districts	Loan Installments Limited and Amount is Heavy		Interest Lost is More		Rigid Bank Policies		Heavy Penalty		Members are Not Prompt		Subsidy Not Allowed		Income Not Growing Fast		Others	
	Nos	%	Nos	%	Nos	%	Nos	%	Nos	%	Nos	%	Nos	%	Nos	%
Bagalkot	9	9.00	34	34.00	25	25.00	13	13.00	34	34.00	18	18.00	32	32.00	11	11.00
Belgaum	8	6.30	76	59.84	4	3.15	6	4.72	46	36.22	51	40.16	24	18.90	8	6.30
Bijapur	17	11.33	37	24.67	49	32.67	21	14.00	41	27.33	24	16.00	35	23.33	15	10.00
Dharwad	8	6.78	51	43.22	17	14.41	15	12.71	42	35.59	27	22.88	33	27.97	9	7.63
Gadag	25	11.36	87	39.55	53	24.09	40	18.18	85	38.64	52	23.64	83	37.73	23	10.45
Haveri	6	7.41	40	49.38	13	16.05	9	11.11	37	45.68	17	20.99	29	35.80	9	11.11
Uttar Kannada	9	8.57	38	36.19	27	25.71	9	8.57	27	25.71	16	15.24	19	18.10	9	8.57
Total	**82**	**9.10**	**363**	**40.29**	**188**	**20.87**	**113**	**12.54**	**312**	**34.63**	**205**	**22.75**	**255**	**28.30**	**84**	**9.32**

Chi-square = 115.2459, P = 0.0000, S

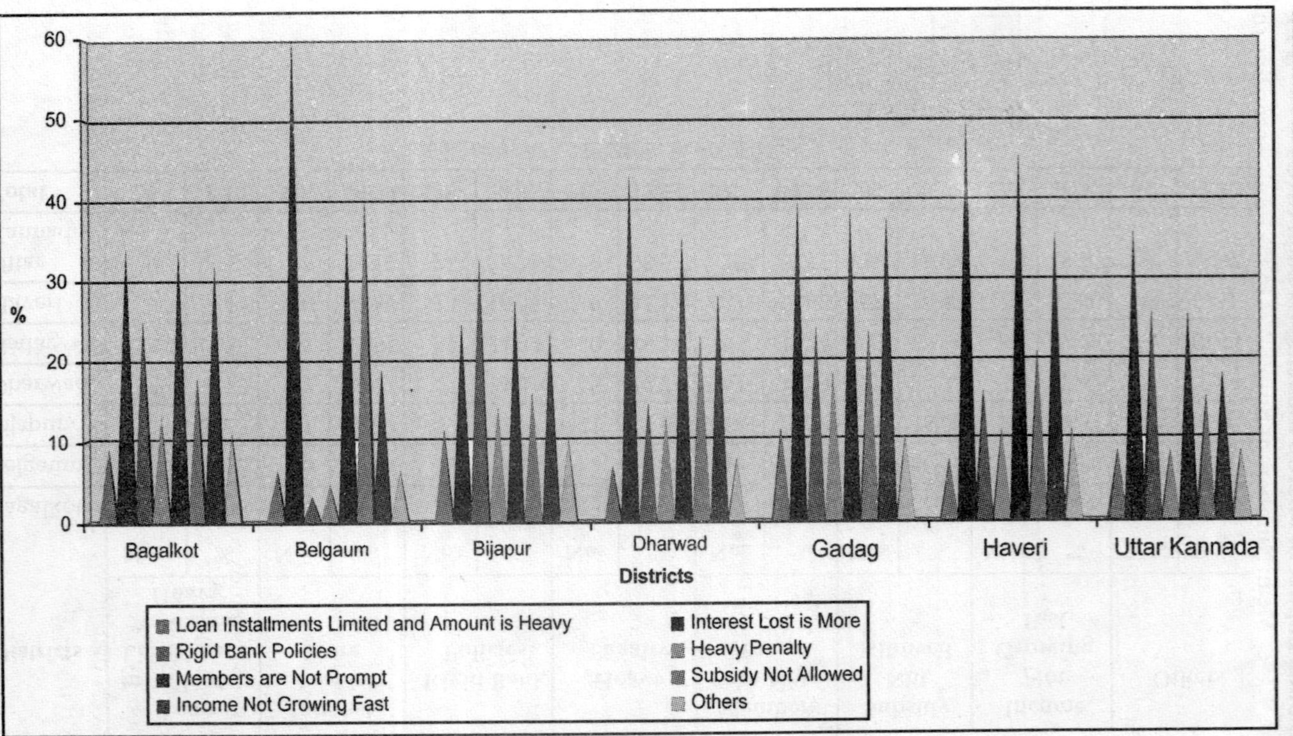

Fig. 4.9: Distribution of Study Samples by Types of Inconveniences

Table 4.36: Mean Numbers of Employees in the Bank According to Different Districts

Districts	Officers	Accountants	Clerks	Others
Bagalkot	2.1	1.0	3.2	2.7
Belgaum	2.0	1.0	2.8	2.4
Bijapur	1.9	1.0	2.4	2.0
Dharwad	1.8	1.0	2.7	2.3
Gadag	2.2	1.0	3.3	2.7
Haveri	1.9	1.0	3.1	2.7
Uttar Kannada	1.9	1.0	2.9	2.4
Total	**2.0**	**1.0**	**2.9**	**2.5**

Table 4.36 depicted the distribution of employees in the bank in the study area on the basis of positions they held. It is indicated from the table that on an average the banks in the study area have two officers, one accountant and three clerks and other staff *i.e.* 2 to 3 depending upon the area in which it is providing services and the volume of business.

Mean Number of SHGs Account in a Branch

The SHGs have to wait for six months to obtain loans from banks. They have to open an account with the nearest branch. The average SHG accounts, savings, bank finance and loan outstanding is shown below. (*See table 4.37 on next page*)

Table 4.37 depicts district-wise mean number of SHG accounts in a branch, total savings deposited in banks, average number of SHGs financed by the bank, total amount financed and loan amount outstanding. Bagalkot district registered highest mean SHG account in banks in the study area. It has 126.8 accounts followed by Gadag with 124.2 and Uttar Kannada with 122.2 mean accounts. Dharwad district has 99.8 mean accounts and Belgaum district is in fifth position by having 95.0 mean accounts. The mean bank accounts in Haveri district were found to be 69.3 and Bijapur is in the last place with 66.6.

Table 4.37: Mean Number of SHGs Account in a Branch and SHGs Obtaining Loans from the Bank

Districts	No. of SHGs Mean Account in a Branch	Savings (Rs.)	No. of SHGs Financed by Bank	Amount Financed (Rs.)	Loan Amount Outstanding (Rs.)
Bagalkot	126.8	372212.3	29.4	2202443.3	1806831.7
Belgaum	95.0	367623.1	28.1	1997760.5	1831925.5
Bijapur	66.6	334319.4	16.7	1064204.9	1056795.4
Dharwad	99.8	443869.5	19.3	1591710.8	1459469.1
Gadag	124.2	414535.7	25.7	2033048.2	1696664.4
Haveri	69.3	297959.8	17.6	1658028.1	1438359.5
Uttar Kannada	122.2	363618.6	29.8	2671534.2	2213972.4
Total	**100.6**	**370591.2**	**23.9**	**1888390.0**	**1655088.6**

Loaning to SHGs by Banks

Banks issue loans to SHGs either directly or through NGOs and by both. The district-wise loaning to SHGs is indicated in the Table 4.38.

Table 4.38: District-wise Loaning to SHGs

District	Directly to SHG		Through NGO		Both		Total
	Nos	%	Nos	%	Nos	%	
Bagalkot	26	52.00	3	6.00	21	42.00	50
Belgaum	31	62.00	4	8.00	15	30.00	50
Bijapur	43	86.00	3	6.00	4	8.00	50
Dharwad	39	78.00	2	4.00	9	18.00	50
Gadag	30	60.00	2	4.00	18	36.00	50
Haveri	32	64.00	2	4.00	16	32.00	50
Uttar Kannada	30	60.00	3	6.00	17	34.00	50
Total	**231**	**66.00**	**19**	**5.43**	**100**	**28.57**	**350**

Table 4.38 shows district-wise loan disbursement to SHGs directly by the banks, through NGOs and by both. Majority of the

banks in all the districts gave loans directly to the SHGs. 66 per cent of the responding banks issued loans directly to SHGs. The percentage of loan has been given through NGOs was found to be 5.43 per cent. Remaining 28.57 per cent loans were disbursed by both directly and through NGOs. This indicates that the banks are in direct touch with SHGs in loan disbursement.

Basis of Determination of Amount of Loans

The determination of loan amount for each SHG largely depends on factors like amount of deposits of the SHG with the bank, need of the loan amount of the SHGs, guidelines of the bank head office, RBI, NABARD and other factors. Among these factors the first factor is usually taken into consideration for the determination of the loan amount by the banks in the study area.

Table 4.39: Basis of Determination of Amount of Loan

District	Amount Deposits		Need of the Loan		Guidelines		Others	
	Nos	%	Nos	%	Nos	%	Nos	%
Bagalkot	38	76.00	10	20.00	7	14.00	3	6.00
Belgaum	32	64.00	15	30.00	11	22.00	2	4.00
Bijapur	35	70.00	10	20.00	20	40.00	0	0.00
Dharwad	32	64.00	12	24.00	12	24.00	0	0.00
Gadag	35	70.00	12	24.00	11	22.00	1	2.00
Haveri	29	58.00	14	28.00	17	34.00	1	2.00
Uttar Kannada	35	70.00	10	20.00	10	20.00	2	4.00
Total	**236**	**67.43**	**83**	**23.71**	**88**	**25.14**	**9**	**2.57**

Table 4.39 depicts that in all the districts majority of banks are considering the amount of deposits of the SHGs with the bank for deciding the loan amount. The percentage of this factor was 67.43 whereas 25.14 per cent of banks determine loan amount on the basis of guidelines of the H. O and 23.71 per cent decides loan amount on need basis. The remaining 2.57 per cent are considering other factors while fixing the loan amount.

Purposes of Loans

The banks are providing loan assistance to SHG for various purposes. Farm operations, small trade, small enterprises, dairying, education, consumption, health, housing, and agricultural instruments are the purposes of loans. The district wise distribution of the study samples on the basis of purpose for which loans are given to SHGs is shown in Table 4.40.

It is observed from Table 4.40 that 322 out of 350 banks surveyed provide loan for small trade, 315 paid loans for dairying, 223 for small business enterprises, 190 for consumption and only 84 for small operation. The other purposes are least considered while issuing loan assistance to SHGs. In Bagalkot district the major purposes of providing loans to SHGs are dairying followed by small trade, small enterprises and consumption. The remaining factors are insignificant. In case of Belgaum district, the main purposes are trade, dairying, small enterprise, consumption and farm operations. The other purposes less considered. Whereas in Bijapur district; trade, Dairying, consumption, small enterprises and farm operations are the major purposes. The percentage of Dharwad district was Trade 98 per cent, small enterprises - 60 per cent consumption 58 per cent and farm operations 18 per cent. The major purposes of loaning to SHGs in Gadag, Haveri, and Uttar Kannada are trade, dairying, small enterprises and consumption. Only small percentage of loan assistance was given to farm operations and others. Health, housing, agricultural equipments purposes are insignificant in loaning to SHGs.

Number of Loan Accounts of SHGs (Total)

The banks have loan accounts of both men and women SHGs. The average loan accounts and average loan amount of men and women is indicated in the Tables 4.41 and 4.42. (*See table on page 119*)

Table 4.41 indicates that the banks have more number of loan accounts of women SHGs in the study area. The average loan accounts of women in the banks were 21.44 and only 2.99 mean number of loan accounts were pertaining to men. Bijapur district has highest with 25.08 average number loan women accounts with the banks. The Bagalkot district has 24.57 mean number of women loan accounts.

Table 4.40: Purposes of Loans to SHGs

Districts	Farm Operations		Small Trade		SSI		Dairying		Education		Con-sumption		Health		Housing		Agricultural Instruments	
	Nos	%	Nos	%	Nos	%	Nos	%	Nos	%	Nos	%	Nos	%	Nos	%	Nos	%
Bagalkot	12	24.00	42	84.00	34	68.00	46	92.00	0	0.00	24	48.00	0	0.00	0	0.00	6	12.00
Belgaum	13	26.00	46	92.00	32	64.00	45	90.00	1	2.00	29	58.00	1	2.00	1	2.00	3	6.00
Bijapur	19	38.00	47	94.00	25	50.00	41	82.00	3	6.00	33	66.00	3	6.00	2	4.00	5	10.00
Dharwad	9	18.00	49	98.00	30	60.00	45	90.00	1	2.00	29	58.00	1	2.00	1	2.00	4	8.00
Gadag	9	18.00	49	98.00	37	74.00	47	94.00	0	0.00	22	44.00	0	0.00	0	0.00	4	8.00
Haveri	11	22.00	42	84.00	29	58.00	45	90.00	0	0.00	27	54.00	1	2.00	0	0.00	5	10.00
Uttar Kannada	11	22.00	47	94.00	36	72.00	46	92.00	0	0.00	26	52.00	1	2.00	0	0.00	4	8.00
Total	**84**	**24.00**	**322**	**92.00**	**223**	**63.71**	**315**	**90.00**	**5**	**1.43**	**190**	**54.29**	**7**	**2.00**	**4**	**1.14**	**31**	**8.86**

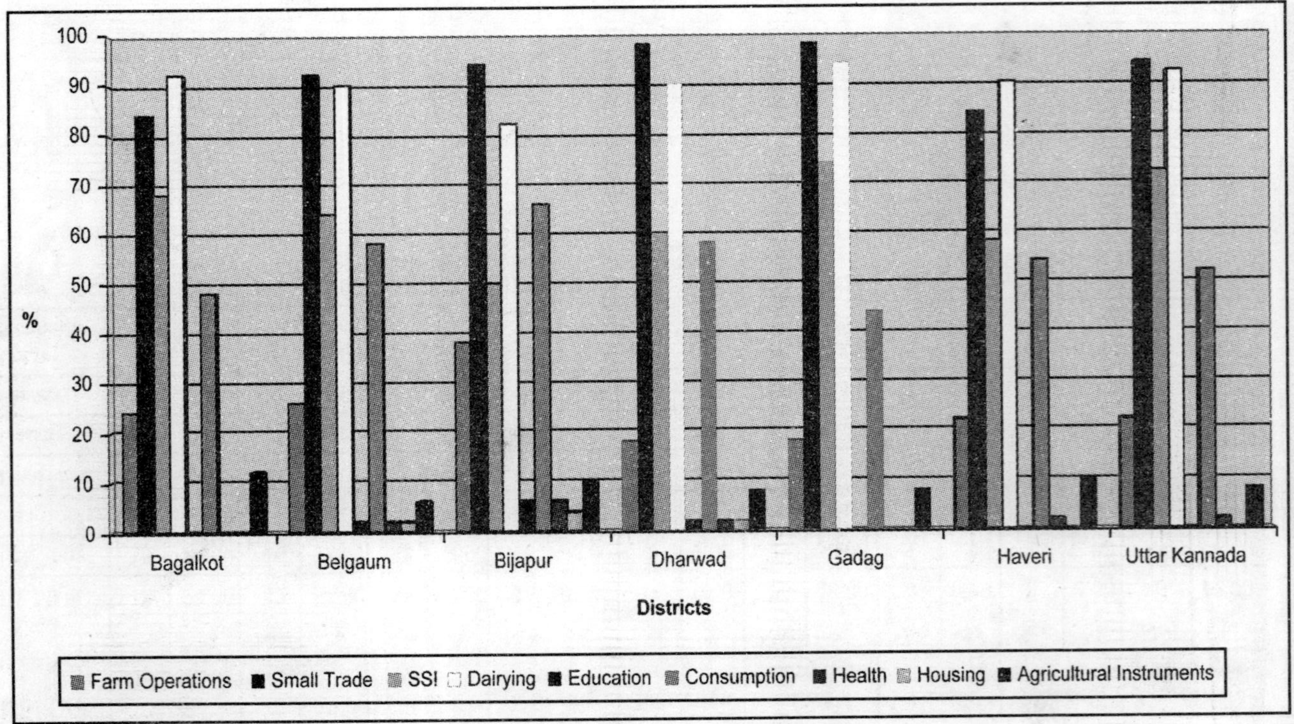

Fig. 4.10: Purposes of Loans to SHGs

Table 4.41: Mean Number of Loan Accounts of SHGs with Banks (No of Samples with Loan Accounts) by Gender and Districts

District	Mean Number of Loan Accounts (Women)	Mean Number of Loan Accounts (Men)
Bagalkot	24.57	2.79
Belgaum	20.13	2.62
Bijapur	25.08	3.85
Dharwad	18.19	2.71
Gadag	19.37	2.50
Haveri	21.26	3.17
Uttar Kannada	21.56	2.50
Total	**21.44**	**2.99**

Uttar Kannada districts has 21.56 and Haveri has 21.26 mean number of women loan accounts. Belgaum, Gadag, and Dharwad districts are having 20.13, 19.37 and 98.19 mean numbers of loan accounts pertaining to women respectively. Again Bijapur district registered highest mean number of men loan accounts of 3.85 followed by Haveri and Bagalkot districts having 3.17 and 2.79 mean number of men loan accounts. The data of Dharwad Belgaum, Gadag and Uttar Kannada were 2.71, 2.62, 2.50 and 2.50 respectively.

Table 4.42: Mean Total Loan Amount to SHGs (Rs. in lakh) by Gender and Districts

District	Mean Total Loan Amount (Women)	Mean Total Loan Amount (Men)
Bagalkot	848068.18	133125.00
Belgaum	604975.61	55217.39
Bijapur	374093.02	97090.91
Dharwad	477681.82	50882.35
Gadag	770113.64	56250.00
Haveri	859488.37	112500.00
Uttar Kannada	965636.36	73500.00
Total	**701498.35**	**83355.93**

Total Loan Amount to SHGs

Since women SHG accounts are more in the banks under study, the total average loan amount to women SHGs was more than the average loan amount of men SHGs. The total average loan amount of women SHGs was Rs. 701498.35 and the men Rs. 8335.50. The Uttar Kannada districts ranks first in the mean total loan amount to women SHG with Rs. 965636.36 l. The Haveri district has Rs. 859488.37. Bagalkot district has Rs. 848068.18; Dharwad district has Rs. 77011364 and Belgaum district with Rs. 604975.61. The mean amount of total loan of Dharwad district was Rs. 477681.82 and Bijapur district was Rs. 374093.02. This clearly shows that women SHGs are dominating in obtaining loan from the banks in the study area.

Purpose-wise Loan

The banks issue loans to SHGs for different purposes. The purpose-wise loan amount to SHGs is shown in the Table 4.43.

It is observed from the Table 4.43 that the major purposes of loan to SHGs in all the districts of the study area are dairying, small trade, small enterprises, and consumption and farm operations. The other reasons are health; education, housing etc. 72.29 per cent of the banks issued loan for dairying. The percentage of the small trade was 66.00, small enterprises - 72.29, consumption - 61.14 and farm operations 55.43. It is clear from the tables that majority of banks in the study area are providing loans for production purposes.

The ratio of average loan amount to SHGs and the average loans of the banks indicate the role of banks in providing the loans to SHGs in the area under study. The mean total loan amount to SHGs and the total loans of the banks and the interest charged by the banks is depicted in Table 4.44 and Table 4.45. (*See tables on page 123*)

Table 4.44 depicts the mean total loan amount to SHGs and total loan amount of the banks in the study area. The average loan amount to SHGs and the total loan amounts of the banks of the entire districts amount to Rs. 1332863.9. Haveri, district registered highest mean total loan amount of Rs. 2467073.2 followed by Bagalkot district amounting to Rs. 1888309.5. The mean loan amount of Uttar Kannada district was Rs. 183675.0 and Belgaum was found to be Rs. 1179463.4. The Gadag, Dharwad and Bijapur districts have Rs. 99340.9, Rs. 19431.8, Rs. 405315.8 mean loan amount respectively.

Table 4.43: Purpose-wise Loan Amount to SHGs

Districts	Farm Operations		Small Trade		SSI		Dairying		Education		Con-sumption		Health		Housing		Agricultural Instruments	
	Nos	%	Nos	%	Nos	%	Nos	%	Nos	%	Nos	%	Nos	%	Nos	%	Nos	%
Bagalkot	28	56.00	34	68.00	30	60.00	36	72.00	1	2.00	38	76.00	4	8.00	1	2.00	22	44.00
Belgaum	29	58.00	34	68.00	35	70.00	36	72.00	3	6.00	27	54.00	4	8.00	2	4.00	24	48.00
Bijapur	21	42.00	30	60.00	28	56.00	32	64.00	5	10.00	15	30.00	6	12.00	4	8.00	10	20.00
Dharwad	27	54.00	30	60.00	32	64.00	36	72.00	5	10.00	30	60.00	9	18.00	4	8.00	17	34.00
Gadag	29	58.00	32	64.00	32	64.00	39	78.00	3	6.00	38	76.00	6	12.00	3	6.00	21	42.00
Haveri	30	60.00	38	76.00	30	60.00	38	76.00	2	4.00	32	64.00	3	6.00	2	4.00	22	44.00
Uttar Kannada	30	60.00	33	66.00	30	60.00	36	72.00	2	4.00	34	68.00	4	8.00	2	4.00	23	46.00
Total	**194**	**55.43**	**231**	**66.00**	**217**	**62.00**	**253**	**72.29**	**21**	**6.00**	**214**	**61.14**	**36**	**10.29**	**18**	**5.14**	**139**	**39.71**

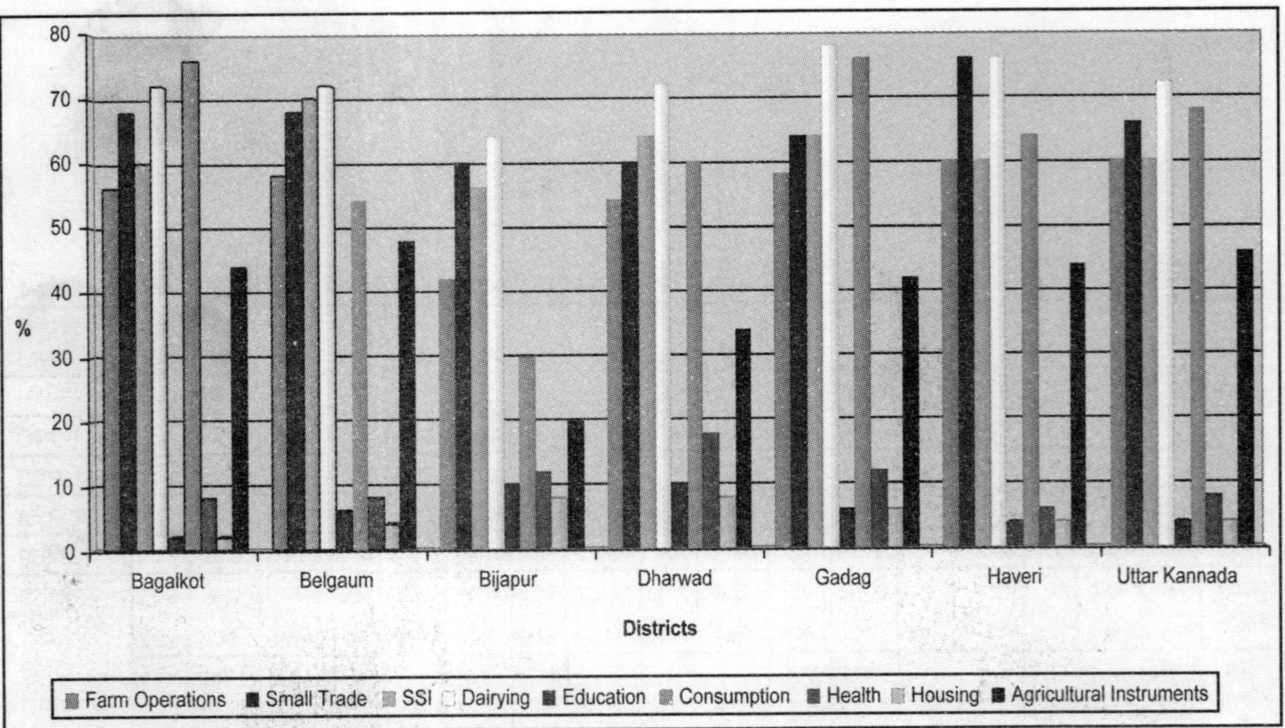

Fig. 4.11: Purpose-wise Loan Amount to SHGs

Table 4.44: Mean Total Loan Amount to SHGs and Total Loans of the Banks (Rs. in lakh)

District	Mean Total Loan Amount to SHGs and Total Loans of the Banks
Bagalkot	1888309.5
Belgaum	1179463.4
Bijapur	405315.8
Dharwad	419431.8
Gadag	1099340.9
Haveri	2467073.2
Uttar Kannada	1836750.0
Total	**1332863.9**

INTEREST ON LOANS

Average Rate of Interest Charged on Loans to SHGs

Table 4.45 depicts average rate of interest charged by the banks on loans to SHGs in the area under study. The average interest rate charged on loans to SHGs varies from district to district. Haveri district registered highest average interest rate of 8.75. The mean rate of interest of Bagalkot district was 8.63. The Uttar Kannada district had 8.50, Belgaum and Gadag districts have 8.25 mean rate of interest, and Belgaum district registered a least of 6.01 mean rate of interest.

Table 4.45: Mean Rate of Interest Charged on Loans to SHGS in Various Districts

District	Mean Rate of Interest Charged on Loans to SHGs
Bagalkot	8.63
Belgaum	8.25
Bijapur	6.01
Dharwad	6.97
Gadag	8.25
Haveri	8.75
Uttar Kannada	8.50
Total	**7.91**

Charging Different Rate of Interest

The banks under study usually charge single rate of interest for different types of loans to SHGs.

Table 4.46: Charging Different Rate of Interest for Different Types of Loans to SHGs

District	Yes	%	No	%	Total
Bagalkot	2	4.00	48	96.00	50
Belgaum	4	8.00	46	92.00	50
Bijapur	7	14.00	43	86.00	50
Dharwad	4	8.00	46	92.00	50
Gadag	1	2.00	49	98.00	50
Haveri	5	10.00	45	90.00	50
Uttar Kannada	4	8.00	46	92.00	50
Total	**27**	**7.71**	**323**	**92.29**	**350**
Chi-square = 6.4216 P = 0.3778, NS					

Table 4.46 shows charging different rate of interest for different type of loans to SHGs by the banks under study. Table clearly indicates that more than 92 per cent of the banks are not charging different rate of interest for different type of loans to SHGs. Only 7.71 per cent of the banks under study are charging different rate of interest for different type of loans. The Chi-Square value is 6.4216 and Pearson's R is 0.3778 indicating no significant relationship between different interest rates charged and type of loans to SHGs.

Documents Obtained from SHGs while Releasing Loan

Banks under study are demanding some documents along with application form while sanctioning loans to SHGs. Bonds, ration card, certificates, photos are some of the documents obtain from the banks. The documents obtained from SHGs while releasing the loan in the area under study is shown in the Table 4.47.

Various documents were demanded by the banks while releasing the loan to SHGs. They are; bonds ration card, certificates and photos of the members of the SHG. It is observed from Table 4.47 that 92 per cent of the banks demand ration card and 90 per cent obtain photo of the SHG members while releasing the loan to SHGs.

Table 4.47: Documents Obtained from SHGs while Releasing Loan

District	Bonds		Ration Card		Certificates		Photo	
	Nos	%	Nos	%	Nos	%	Nos	%
Bagalkot	12	24.00	42	84.00	34	68.00	46	92.00
Belgaum	13	26.00	46	92.00	32	64.00	45	90.00
Bijapur	19	38.00	47	94.00	25	50.00	41	82.00
Dharwad	9	18.00	49	98.00	30	60.00	45	90.00
Gadag	9	18.00	49	98.00	37	74.00	47	94.00
Haveri	11	22.00	42	84.00	29	58.00	45	90.00
Uttar Kannada	11	22.00	47	94.00	36	72.00	46	92.00
Total	**84**	**24.00**	**322**	**92.00**	**223**	**63.71**	**315**	**90.00**

63.71 per cent obtain certificates and 24 per cent demand bonds. This clearly indicates that photos for identification of SHG members and ration card for address proof are necessary conditions for the release of loan.

Details of Repeat Loan Disbursed by Branch

Banks are studying the credit requirements of the members, timely repayment of earlier loans and member's involvement in income-generation activities to sanction the repeat loans. The repeat loans disbursed by the branch in different districts are depicted in the Table 4.48.

Table 4.48: Repeat Loans Disbursed by Branch in Different Districts during 2005-09

District	Repeat Mean Loan in 2005-06	Repeat Mean Loan in 2006-07	Repeat Mean Loan in 2007-08	Repeat Mean Loan in 2008-09
Bagalkot	41087.0	88655.2	-111206.9	138088.2
Belgaum	40136.4	79000.0	87941.2	104324.3
Bijapur	37505.0	72222.0	57357.0	81052.0
Dharwad	34608.7	61030.3	68625.0	83409.1
Gadag	37173.9	69212.1	81285.7	119166.7
Haveri	32437.5	61391.3	63125.0	101451.6
Uttar Kannada	55291.7	110781.3	125806.5	163375.0
Total	**40179.3**	**77967.2**	**84096.6**	**112744.3**

Table 4.48 depicts that the mean repeat loan has been showing an increasing trend during 2005-09. In 2005-06 the mean repeat loan of the entire district was found to be Rs. 40179.3 and it has been increased to Rs. 112744.3 in 2007. This shows that the banks are interested in providing repeat loans to SHGs in the area under study. During 2009 Uttar Kannada district registered highest mean repeat loan of Rs. 163375.0 followed by Bagalkot and Gadag districts with Rs. 138088.2 and Rs. 119166.7 respectively. The mean repeat loan of Belgaum, Haveri, Dharwad and Bijapur was found to be Rs. 104324.3, Rs. 101451.6, Rs. 83409 and Rs. 81052 respectively.

Time Taken by the Bank in Releasing Loan

Table 4.49 shows that, about 56.57 per cent of banks in the study area are taking two weeks time, 32.29 per cent of the banks are disbursing the loan in one week and the remaining 11.14 per cents banks need more than two weeks. 80 per cent of the banks in Bijapur district are taking two weeks time in releasing the loan. It is inferred from the Table 4.49 that there is a significant relationship between usual times taken by the banks and releasing the loan amount after receiving the applications from SHGs as the Chi-Square value is 21.3252 and Pearson's R is 0.0458.

Table 4.49: Details of Time Taken by the Bank in Releasing Loan Amount after Receiving the Applications

District	One Week	%	Two Weeks	%	>Two Weeks	%	Total
Bagalkot	19	38.00	25	50.00	6	12.00	50
Belgaum	20	40.00	27	54.00	3	6.00	50
Bijapur	8	16.00	40	80.00	2	4.00	50
Dharwad	12	24.00	29	58.00	9	18.00	50
Gadag	15	30.00	27	54.00	8	16.00	50
Haveri	21	42.00	24	48.00	5	10.00	50
Uttar Kannada	18	36.00	26	52.00	6	12.00	50
Total	**113**	**32.29**	**198**	**56.57**	**39**	**11.14**	**350**

Chi-square = 21.3252, P = 0.0458, S

Fixing Maximum Limit of Loan for Different Purposes

Banks adopt their own policies while issuing loans for different purposes. Some banks fix maximum limit for different purposes while others are not. Fixing maximum limit of loan for Different Purposes of SHGs is indicated in the Table 4.50 and Table 4.51.

Table 4.50: Fixing Maximum Limit of Loan for Different Purposes of SHGs

District	Yes	%	No	%	Total
Bagalkot	5	10.00	45	90.00	50
Belgaum	6	12.00	44	88.00	50
Bijapur	10	20.00	40	80.00	50
Dharwad	12	24.00	38	76.00	50
Gadag	7	14.00	43	86.00	50
Haveri	10	20.00	40	80.00	50
Uttar Kannada	6	12.00	44	88.00	50
Total	**56**	**16.00**	**294**	**84.00**	**350**
Chi-square = 6.2504 P = 0.3964, NS					

The fixing maximum limit of loan for different purposes of SHGs in the study area is indicated in the Table 4.50. Table 4.50 indicates that, majority of the banks in all the district of the study area expressed that they do not fix maximum limit of loan for different purposes of SHGs. 84 per cent gave negative response and remaining 16 per cent banks said that they are fixing the maximum limit of loan for different purposes. This shows that the loan amount is provided on need basis and the amount applied far. The Chi-Square value is 6.2504 and Pearson's R is 0.3964 indicating no significant relationship between fixing maximum limit and purpose of SHGs in obtaining loan.

Table 4.51 depicts the purposes of fixing maximum limit of loan for different purposes for SHGs in the study area. Table shows that the surveyed branches gave positive response. 36 branches agreed that they are fixing the maximum limit loan to small enterprises, 23 branches for small trade, 17 branches marked dairying and 20 branches responded for other reasons. Only 6 branches expressed with regards to farm operation.

Table 4.51: Fixing-up Maximum Limit of Loan for Different Purposes for SHGs

District	Farm Operations	Small Trade	SSI	Dairying	Others
Bagalkot	0	1	5	1	0
Belgaum	1	1	2	0	4
Bijapur	2	5	5	3	5
Dharwad	1	7	7	6	5
Gadag	0	4	5	4	2
Haveri	1	2	7	1	3
Uttar Kannada	1	3	5	2	1
Total	**6**	**23**	**36**	**17**	**20**

Banks under study usually keep annual target number and amount of loan finance to SHGs.

The district-wise Banks fixing the target of loan finance to SHGs every year under the study area is shown in the Table 4.52.

Table 4.52: Bank Fix Target of Loan Finance to SHGs Every Year

District	Yes	%	No	%	Total
Bagalkot	50	100.00	0	0.00	50
Belgaum	49	98.00	1	2.00	50
Bijapur	48	96.00	2	4.00	50
Dharwad	49	98.00	1	2.00	50
Gadag	50	100.00	0	0.00	50
Haveri	50	100.00	0	0.00	50
Uttar Kannada	50	100.00	0	0.00	50
Total	**346**	**98.86**	**4**	**1.14**	**350**

Table 4.52 indicates that the major portion of banks kept the target numbers, target amount of loan finance to SHGs every year. Around 99 per cent of the banks gave positive response. Hardly 1 per cent of the banks have shown negative response.

Reasons for Falling Short of the Target Amount

Though, banks keeping the target, some branches do not reach the target number and amount every year. Fewer loan applications, lower amount demanded by the SHGs, delay in processing of applications and others are some of the reasons for falling short of the target amount. The reasons for the falling short of the target amount are shown below. (Table 4.53)

Table 4.53: Reasons for Falling Short of the Target Amount

District	Lower Amount Applied		Less Number of Loan Application		Delay in Processing of Applications		Others	
	Nos	%	Nos	%	Nos	%	Nos	%
Bagalkot	26	52.00	33	66.00	8	16.00	28	56.00
Belgaum	12	24.49	23	46.94	1	2.04	34	69.39
Bijapur	11	22.92	37	77.08	3	6.25	4	8.33
Dharwad	16	32.65	24	48.98	18	36.73	11	22.45
Gadag	16	32.00	35	70.00	5	10.00	13	26.00
Haveri	12	24.00	40	80.00	3	6.00	10	20.00
Uttar Kannada	16	32.00	39	78.00	2	4.00	14	28.00
Total	**109**	**31.50**	**231**	**66.76**	**40**	**11.56**	**114**	**32.95**
Chi-square = 86.5465 P = 0.0000, S								

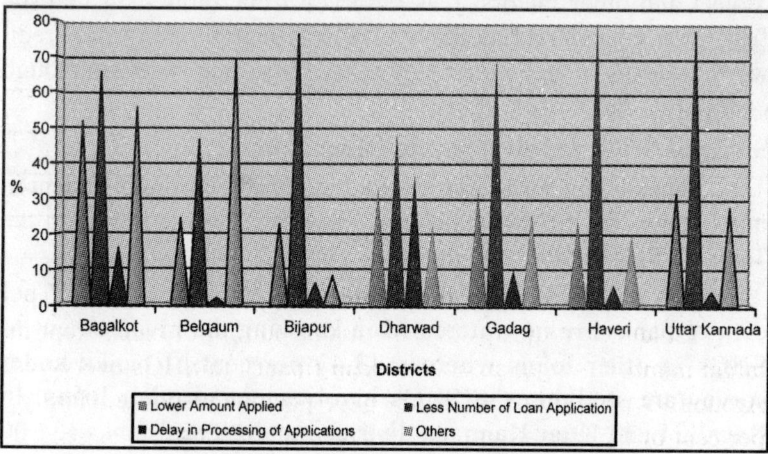

Fig. 4.12: Reasons for Falling Short of the Target Amount

Table 4.53 indicates the reasons for falling short of the target amount kept by the banks in the area under study. Table 4.53 depicts that the major reason for short of the target is less number of applications received for loan followed by other reasons and the amount applied by SHGs was lower than the target. Delay in processing of applications of SHGs reason is insignificant in the study area. The Chi-Square value is 86.5465 and Pearson's R is 0.0000 indicating a significant relationship between loaning the SHGs and reasons for falling short of the target amount.

Pre-sanction Measures

Making on the spot study of the project and its validity, surety's financial soundness, encashment feasibility, checking legal documents, obtaining project details are some of the steps taken by the banks while estimating the credit worthiness and credit needs of the borrowers. Table 4.54 indicates Steps Taken by Banks while Estimating the Credit Worthiness and Credit Needs of the Borrowers.

The banks while assessing the credit worthiness and credit needs of the borrowers are taking in to consideration the project details of the SHG investment, making on the spot study of the project and its viability, financial sources of the SHGs, surety's financial soundness, encashment feasibility of the securities, assessing the assets of the SHGs, checking the legal documents pertaining to the project and other factors. It is observed from Table 4.54 that the first three considerations plays vital role in estimating the credit worthiness in the area under study. The remaining steps are though considered, but not significant.

Study of SHGs Involvement in Other Loans

Banks in the study area are studying the SHGs involvement in other loans. The SHGs involvement in other loans is shown in the Table 4.55. (*See table on page 133*)

It is observed from the Table 4.55 that around 56.57 per cent of banks are not interested in knowing the involvement of SHGs in other loans whereas 43.43 per cent of banks under survey are studying the SHGs involvement in other loans. In Bagalkot and Uttar Kannada districts, majority of banks (54.00 and 52.00%) studying the involvement of SHGs in other loans.

Table 4.54: Steps Taken by Banks while Estimating the Credit Worthiness and Credit Needs of the Borrowers

Districts	Project Details		Making on the Spot Study		Financial Sources of the SHGs		Surety's Financial Soundness		Encashment Feasibility of he Surety		Checking the Legal Documents	
	Nos	%	Nos	%	Nos	%	Nos	%	Nos	%	Nos	%
Bagalkot	37	74.00	34	68.00	32	64.00	20	40.00	4	8.00	8	16.00
Belgaum	36	72.00	35	70.00	28	56.00	18	36.00	2	4.00	12	24.00
Bijapur	30	60.00	35	70.00	35	70.00	4	8.00	1	2.00	3	6.00
Dharwad	38	76.00	36	72.00	29	58.00	9	18.00	0	0.00	9	18.00
Gadag	40	80.00	33	66.00	35	70.00	14	28.00	1	2.00	8	16.00
Haveri	40	80.00	37	74.00	32	64.00	18	36.00	5	10.00	10	20.00
Uttar Kannada	40	80.00	35	70.00	33	66.00	14	28.00	2	4.00	9	18.00
Total	**261**	**74.57**	**245**	**70.00**	**224**	**64.00**	**97**	**27.71**	**15**	**4.29**	**59**	**16.86**

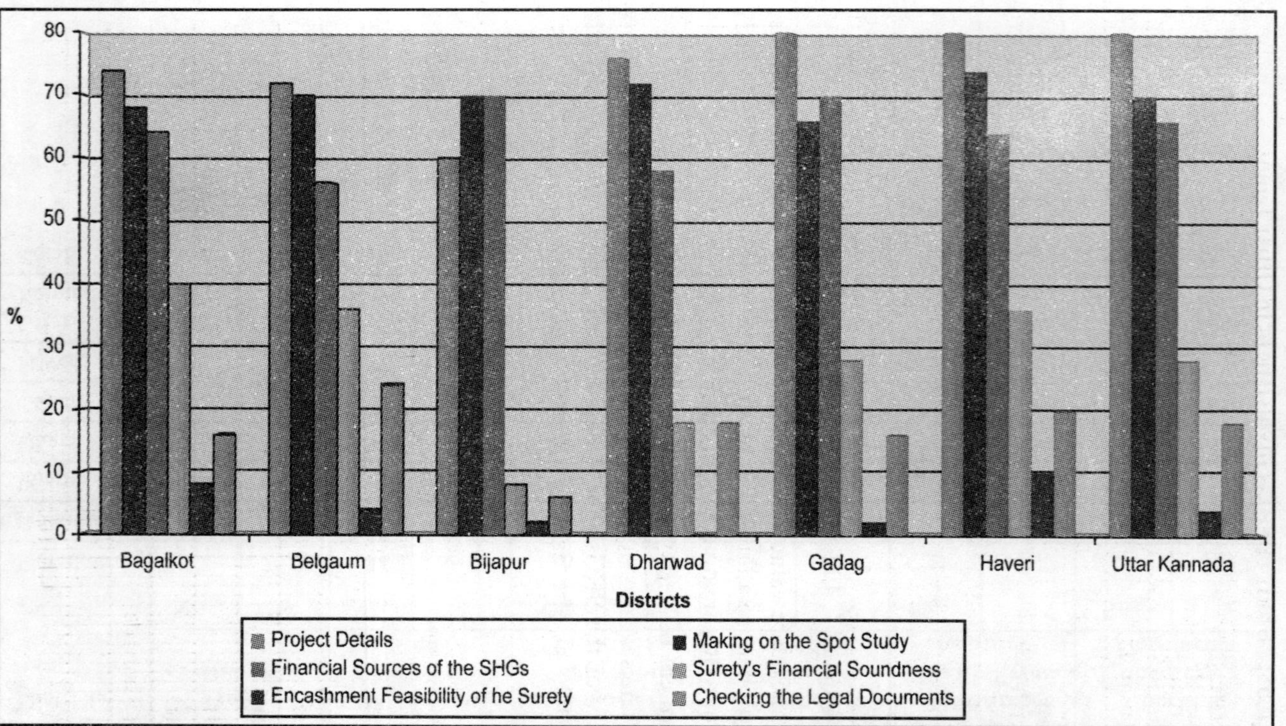

Fig. 4.13: Steps Taken by Banks while Estimating the Credit Worthiness and Credit Needs of the Borrowers

Table 4.55: Study of SHGs Involvement in Other Loans

District	Yes	%	No	%	Total
Bagalkot	27	54.00	23	46.00	50
Belgaum	18	36.00	32	64.00	50
Bijapur	21	42.00	29	58.00	50
Dharwad	15	30.00	35	70.00	50
Gadag	22	44.00	28	56.00	50
Haveri	23	46.00	27	54.00	50
Uttar Kannada	26	52.00	24	48.00	50
Total	**152**	**43.43**	**198**	**56.57**	**350**
Chi-square = 8.7453 P = 0.1883, NS					

The Chi-Square value is 8.7453 and Pearson's R is 0.1883 showing no significant relationship between sanction of loans to SHGs and study of SHGs involvement in other loans.

Assessment of Repayment Capacity

Banks while releasing the loans to SHGs assess the repayment capacity of the SHGs. The Assessment of Repayment Capacity of the SHGs by the banks in the study area is indicated in the Table 4.56.

Table 4.56: Assessment of Repayment Capacity of the SHGs

District	Yes	%	No	%	Total
Bagalkot	8	16.00	42	84.00	50
Belgaum	3	6.00	47	94.00	50
Bijapur	1	2.00	49	98.00	50
Dharwad	2	4.00	48	96.00	50
Gadag	6	12.00	44	88.00	50
Haveri	7	14.00	43	86.00	50
Uttar Kannada	9	18.00	41	82.00	50
Total	**36**	**10.29**	**314**	**89.71**	**350**
Chi-square = 12.7572 P = 0.0472, S					

Table 4.56 clearly shows that around 90 per cent of the banks in all the districts of the area under study are not assessing the repayment capacity of the SHGs. Only 10 per cent of the SHGs are interested in assessing the repayment capacity. In Uttar Kannada and Bagalkot districts the percentage of assessment is more pronounced *i.e.* 18 and 16 per cent respectively. There is a significant relationship between sanction of loans to SHGs and its repayment capacity since the Chi-Square value is 12.7572 and Pearson's R is 0.0472.

Utilisation of Loan by SHGs

Banks used to enforce the proper utilisation of loan by the SHGs in the study area. The enforcement of proper utilisation of loan by the SHGs is shown in the Table 4.57.

Table 4.57: Enforcement of Proper Utilisation of Loan by the SHGs

District	Yes	%	No	%	Total
Bagalkot	45	90.00	5	10.00	50
Belgaum	47	94.00	3	6.00	50
Bijapur	50	100.00	0	0.00	50
Dharwad	50	100.00	0	0.00	50
Gadag	47	94.00	3	6.00	50
Haveri	47	94.00	3	6.00	50
Uttar Kannada	48	96.00	2	4.00	50
Total	**334**	**95.43**	**16**	**4.57**	**350**

Table 4.57 clearly shows that more than 95 per cent banks in all the districts of the study area enforce proper utilisation of the loan by the SHG's hardly less than 5 per cent banks do not enforce.

Release of Next Loan

Repeat loans will be given only to those SHGs which have repaid the installment in time. The release of next loan only after the first loan is properly utilised, instances of miss-utilisation, per cent of loan diverted and the type of SHGs diverted loans are shown in the Tables 4.58, 4.59, 4.60 and 4.61.

Table 4.58: Release of Next Loan Only after First Loan is Properly Utilised

District	Yes	%	No	%	Total
Bagalkot	50	100.00	0	0.00	50
Belgaum	50	100.00	0	0.00	50
Bijapur	47	94.00	3	6.00	50
Dharwad	49	98.00	1	2.00	50
Gadag	50	100.00	0	0.00	50
Haveri	50	100.00	0	0.00	50
Uttar Kannada	50	100.00	0	0.00	50
Total	**346**	**98.86**	**4**	**1.14**	**350**

Chi-square = 13.6526 P = 0.0334, S

The release of next loan only after first loan is promptly utilised in the area under study is shown in Table 4.58. Almost 99 per cent of the banks in all the districts of the study area release next loan only after first loan are properly utilised. Hardly 1.14 per cent gave negative response. The Chi-Square value is 13.6526 and Pearson's R is 0.0334 showing a significant relationship between release of next loan and utilisation of the first loan.

Table 4.59: Instance of Miss-utilisation

District	Yes	%	No	%	Total
Bagalkot	8	16.00	42	84.00	50
Belgaum	3	6.00	47	94.00	50
Bijapur	1	2.00	49	98.00	50
Dharwad	2	4.00	48	96.00	50
Gadag	6	12.00	44	88.00	50
Haveri	7	14.00	43	86.00	50
Uttar Kannada	9	18.00	41	82.00	50
Total	**36**	**10.29**	**314**	**89.71**	**350**

Instance of Miss-utilisation

Table 4.59 shows the instance of miss-utilisation or diversion of loan funds for other purposes in the study area. Table 4.59 shows that 89.71 per cent of the respondents in the area under study expressed that the loan amount provided to SHGs was properly utilised. The remaining 10.29 per cent of the respondents found the instances of miss-utilisation.

Table 4.60: Per cent of Loan Diverted or Miss-utilised

District	<2 %	%	2-5 %	%	5-8 %	%	8-10 %	%	>10 %	%	Total
Bagalkot	30	60.0	14	28.0	3	6.0	3	6.0	0	0.0	50
Belgaum	17	34.0	15	30.0	14	28.0	4	8.0	0	0.0	50
Bijapur	14	28.0	20	40.0	13	26.0	2	4.0	1	2.0	50
Dharwad	16	32.0	13	26.0	16	32.0	5	10.0	0	0.0	50
Gadag	25	50.0	15	30.0	6	12.0	4	8.0	0	0.0	50
Haveri	26	52.0	13	26.0	9	18.0	2	4.0	0	0.0	50
Uttar Kannada	29	58.0	13	26.0	5	10.0	3	6.0	0	0.0	50
Total	**157**	**44.9**	**103**	**29.4**	**66**	**18.9**	**23**	**6.6**	**1**	**0.3**	**350**

Loan Diverted or Miss-utilised

The per cent of loan diverted or miss-utilised in the study area is depicted in the Table 4.60. It is seen from the Table 4.60 that, 157 (44.9%) out of 350 respondents opined that less than 2 per cent of loan was diverted or miss-utilised. 29.4 per cent of the respondents said that the percentage of diversion or miss-utilisation was 2-5 per cent.

Table 4.61: Type of SHGs Diverted Bank Loan

District	Yes	%	No	%	Total
Bagalkot	12	24.00	38	76.00	50
Belgaum	6	12.00	44	88.00	50
Bijapur	3	6.00	47	94.00	50
Dharwad	5	10.00	45	90.00	50
Gadag	7	14.00	43	86.00	50
Haveri	11	22.00	39	78.00	50
Uttar Kannada	9	18.00	41	82.00	50
Total	53	15.14	297	84.86	350
Chi-square = 9.9172 P = 0.1283, NS					

The percentage of miss-utilisation under 5-8 per cent category was 18.9 and 6.6 percentage of respondents agree that the percentage of miss-utilisation was 8-10. The percentage of diversion or miss-utilisation is more than 10 per cent category is negligible in the study area.

Table 4.61 indicates the type of the SHGs diverted the loan in the study area. It is evident from the Table 4.61 that 84.86 per cent of the men SHGs have diverted the loan and hardly 15.14 per cent of the women SHGs diverted the bank loan in the area under study. The Chi-Square value is 9.9172 and Pearson's R is 0.1283 showing a significant relationship between type of SHGs (Men and Women) and diversion of bank loans.

Periodical Inspections of SHGs

Banks under study conducts periodical inspection after the loan issued to SHGs and enforces proper utilisation. The periodical inspection of SHGs is depicted in the Table 4.62.

Table 4.62: Periodical Inspections of SHGs

District	Yes	%	No	%	Total
Bagalkot	40	80.00	10	20.00	50
Belgaum	43	86.00	7	14.00	50
Bijapur	47	94.00	3	6.00	50
Dharwad	39	78.00	11	22.00	50
Gadag	39	78.00	11	22.00	50
Haveri	44	88.00	6	12.00	50
Uttar Kannada	42	84.00	8	16.00	50
Total	**294**	**84.00**	**56**	**16.00**	**350**
Chi-square = 7.7381 P = 0.2582, NS					

Table 4.62 show that majority of the banks in the study area have made periodical inspection of the SHGs. The percentage of periodical inspection by the banks was found to be 84 and the remaining 16 per cent said that they do not conduct any periodical inspection. It is depicted from the table that there is no significant relationship between periodical inspections of SHGs and assessing the utilisation of loans as the Chi-Square value is 7.7381 and Pearson's R is 0.2582.

Incidence of Miss-utilisation

SGSY, SJSRY, Sthree-Shakthi and SHG bank linkage are some government programmes which are initiated for the alleviation of poverty in rural areas. The incidence of miss-utilisation under Government sponsored Programmes is shown in the Table 4.63.

Table 4.63: Incidence of Miss-utilisation under Government Sponsored Programmes

District	SGSY		SJSRY		SS		Others		Total
	Nos	%	Nos	%	Nos	%	Nos	%	
Bagalkot	37	74.00	11	22.00	2	4.00	0	0.00	50
Belgaum	26	52.00	23	46.00	1	2.00	0	0.00	50
Bijapur	18	36.00	31	62.00	0	0.00	1	2.00	50
Dharwad	30	60.00	20	40.00	0	0.00	0	0.00	50
Gadag	38	76.00	11	22.00	1	2.00	0	0.00	50
Haveri	29	58.00	18	36.00	3	6.00	0	0.00	50
Uttar Kannada	37	74.00	11	22.00	2	4.00	0	0.00	50
Total	**215**	**61.43**	**125**	**35.71**	**9**	**2.57**	**1**	**0.29**	**350**

The incidence of miss-utilisation under SGSY was more than SJSRY and Stree Shakti. Table 4.63 clearly indicates that the incidence of miss-utilisation is more pronounced in SGSY Scheme followed by SJSRY in the Study area. The incidence of miss-utilisation in SGSY is 61.43 per cent; SJSRY 35.71 per cent, Stree Shakti 2.57 per cent and other programmes is hardly 0.29 per cent.

Recovery of Loan from SHGs

Banks recover the amount of loan from the SHGs in installments. The mean number of loan repayment installments, fixation of loan installments and fixing different number of installments for loans to different purpose are indicated in the Tables 4.64, 4.65 and 4.66.

Table 4.64 depicts the mean number of loan repayment installments fixed by the banks for the SHGs in the study area. The total mean number of installment was 35.51 Bagalkot district has (40.89) highest mean number of installment followed by Haveri, Gadag, Uttar Kannada and Belgaum districts. The Dharwad and

Table 4.64: Mean Numbers of Installments

District	Mean Number of Installments
Bagalkot	40.09
Belgaum	33.31
Bijapur	26.88
Dharwad	31.20
Gadag	38.88
Haveri	39.92
Uttar Kannada	38.64
Total	**35.51**

and Bijapur districts have 31.20 and 26.88 mean number of installments respectively. This clearly shows that, usually the banks provide 30 to 36 monthly installments to repay the loan in the study area.

Fixing Installments

Table 4.65 depicts the persons fixing the installments in the area under study. Majority of the banks under study except Haveri district fix the installments on the basis of head office instructions and in some banks the installments are fixed by the bank manager. In Haveri districts banks fixing loan installments on the basis of head office guidelines and directly by the manager and only few banks consider the guidelines of RBI and NABARD.

Table 4.65: Fixing Installments

District	Bank Manager		Bank HO		Guidelines of NABARD/RBI		Total
	Nos	%	Nos	%	Nos	%	
Bagalkot	15	30.00	37	74.00	8	16.00	50
Belgaum	15	30.00	41	82.00	9	18.00	50
Bijapur	8	16.00	45	90.00	8	16.00	50
Dharwad	9	18.00	44	88.00	7	14.00	50
Gadag	12	24.00	41	82.00	8	16.00	50
Haveri	23	46.00	32	64.00	15	30.00	50
Uttar Kannada	15	30.00	38	76.00	9	18.00	50
Total	**97**	**27.71**	**278**	**79.43**	**64**	**18.29**	**350**

Table 4.66: Fixing Different Number of Installments for Loans to Different Purposes

District	Yes	%	No	%	Total
Bagalkot	8	16.00	42	84.00	50
Belgaum	6	12.00	44	88.00	50
Bijapur	4	8.00	46	92.00	50
Dharwad	6	12.00	44	88.00	50
Gadag	8	16.00	42	84.00	50
Haveri	10	20.00	40	80.00	50
Uttar Kannada	6	12.00	44	88.00	50
Total	**48**	**13.71**	**302**	**86.29**	**350**

Fixation of different number of installments for loan repayment for loans to different category in the area under study is shown in the Table 4.66. More than 86 per cent of the banks in the study area do not fix different number of installments for loans to different categories. Only 13.71 per cent banks fix the different number of installments for loans to different purposes.

Repayment of Loan by SHGs

The performance of the repayment of the SHGs in the area under study was found to be prompt and satisfactory. Only small percentage delayed the repayment of loans. The repayment of loan by the SHGs is depicted in the Table 4.67.

Table 4.67: Repayment of Loan by SHGs

District	Prompt	%	Satisfactory	%	Delayed	%	Total
Bagalkot	32	64.00	11	22.00	7	14.00	50
Belgaum	31	62.00	16	32.00	3	6.00	50
Bijapur	25	50.00	25	50.00	0	0.00	50
Dharwad	26	52.00	20	40.00	4	8.00	50
Gadag	30	60.00	12	24.00	8	16.00	50
Haveri	25	50.00	18	36.00	7	14.00	50
Uttar Kannada	31	62.00	11	22.00	8	16.00	50
Total	**200**	**57.14**	**113**	**32.29**	**37**	**10.57**	**350**

Table 4.67 clearly indicates that 57.14 per cent of the SHGs in the area under study are prompt, 32.39 per cent are found to be satisfactory and only 10.57 per cent make delay in the repayment of loans. This indicates that the recovery rate was found very well in the study area.

Steps Taken

Sending reminders, telephone reminders, issuing notices, issuing legal notices, seizing property and filing legal suits are some of the steps taken by the banks for recovery of loans from SHGs in the study area. Table 4.68 indicates steps taken for recovery of loans from SHGs. (*See table 4.68 on next page*)

The major steps taken in the study area are; sending reminders, telephone reminders and issuing notices. The remaining measures for the recovery of loan from the SHGs are insignificant. The Chi-Square value is 20.4800 and Pearson's R is 0.9033 showing a significant relationship between recovery of loans and steps taken by the banks for recovery of loans from SHGs.

Training of SHGs

Major portion of the members of the SHGs are illiterates in the study area. Hence, they need training in various areas. The Government directly or through NGOs has to provide training to the members. Some banks in the area under study involved indirectly in training and most of the banks feel that training is necessary before financing the SHGs. The bank involvement in the training of SHGs and consideration of training before financing the SHGs are shown in the Table 4.69 and Table 4.70. (*See tables on page 143*)

Table 4.69 indicates the banks involvement in training of SHGs in the area under study. It is observed from the table that, 79.71 per cent of the banks in the study area are not involved in the training of SHGs. Remaining 20.29 per cent of the banks were involved in training.

The training of SHGs as criteria before financing SHGs in the study area is depicted in the Table 4.70. It is observed from the table that 94.86 per cent respondents expressed that training is necessary whereas only 5.14 per cent banks opined that training is not necessary. The Chi-Square value is 11.3629 and Pearson's R is 0.0798 showing a significant relationship between training considerations and financing to SHGs.

Table 4.68: Steps Taken for Recovery of Loans from SHGs

Districts	Sending Reminders		Telephone Reminders		Issuing Notices		Issuing Legal Notices		Seizing Property		Filing Legal Suits	
	Nos	%	Nos	%	Nos	%	Nos	%	Nos	%	Nos	%
Bagalkot	47	94.00	39	78.00	13	26.00	5	10.00	6	12.00	5	10.00
Belgaum	48	96.00	42	84.00	13	26.00	3	6.00	8	16.00	3	6.00
Bijapur	47	94.00	47	94.00	9	18.00	0	0.00	6	12.00	0	0.00
Dharwad	49	98.00	43	86.00	16	32.00	3	6.00	12	24.00	3	6.00
Gadag	48	96.00	43	86.00	20	40.00	4	8.00	14	28.00	4	8.00
Haveri	49	98.00	39	78.00	19	38.00	4	8.00	11	22.00	4	8.00
Uttar Kannada	49	98.00	41	82.00	19	38.00	4	8.00	11	22.00	4	8.00
Total	**337**	**96.29**	**294**	**84.00**	**109**	**31.14**	**23**	**6.57**	**68**	**19.43**	**23**	**6.57**

Chi-square = 20.4800 P = 0.9033, NS

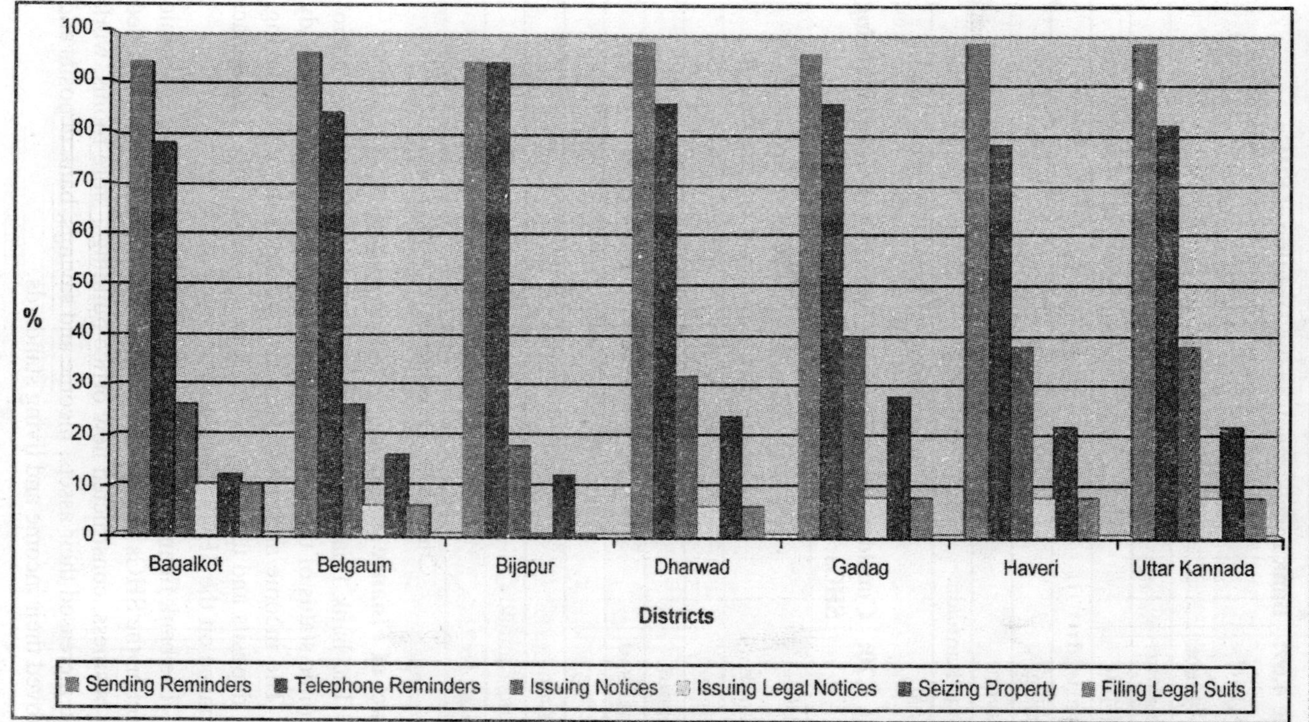

Fig. 4.14: Steps Taken for Recovery of Loans from SHGs

Table 4.69: Bank Involvements in the Training of SHGs

District	Yes	%	No	%	Total
Bagalkot	15	30.00	35	70.00	50
Belgaum	11	22.00	39	78.00	50
Bijapur	5	10.00	45	90.00	50
Dharwad	9	18.00	41	82.00	50
Gadag	11	22.00	39	78.00	50
Haveri	9	18.00	41	82.00	50
Uttar Kannada	11	22.00	39	78.00	50
Total	**71**	**20.29**	**279**	**79.71**	**350**

Table 4.70: Consideration of Training Necessary Before Financing SHGs

District	Yes	%	No	%	Total
Bagalkot	44	88.00	6	12.00	50
Belgaum	48	96.00	2	4.00	50
Bijapur	46	92.00	4	8.00	50
Dharwad	50	100.00	0	0.00	50
Gadag	49	98.00	1	2.00	50
Haveri	46	92.00	4	8.00	50
Uttar Kannada	49	98.00	1	2.00	50
Total	**332**	**94.86**	**18**	**5.14**	**350**

Chi-square = 11.3629 P = 0.0798, NS

Impact of Finance on SHGs

The bank finance has made a greater implication on socio-economic status of the rural poor especially the women in the study area. The income and living standard has been improved, saving, bank deposits and use of assets increased considerably. The impact of finance on the SHGs is depicted in the Table 4.71.

The bank finance to SHGs has made greater positive economic impact on the SHGs and members under study. SHGs have expanded their business, constructed new office buildings, store rooms, work ships, increased their assets, income and savings, bank deposits and improved their income and living standards.

Table 4.71: Impact of Finance on SHGs

Districts	SHGs Expanded their Business		Constructed New Office Buildings		Storerooms and Workshops		Increased their Assets		Interest in Savings		Increase in Bank Deposits		Increase in Income		Increase in Living Standard	
	Nos	%	Nos	%	Nos	%	Nos	%	Nos	%	Nos	%	Nos	%	Nos	%
Bagalkot	42	84.00	0	0.00	0	0.00	35	70.00	39	78.00	36	72.00	32	64.00	34	68.00
Belgaum	45	90.00	0	0.00	0	0.00	42	84.00	34	68.00	24	48.00	27	54.00	40	80.00
Bijapur	48	96.00	1	2.00	0	0.00	43	86.00	24	48.00	16	32.00	11	22.00	48	96.00
Dharwad	47	94.00	0	0.00	0	0.00	43	86.00	25	50.00	16	32.00	17	34.00	42	84.00
Gadag	43	86.00	0	0.00	0	0.00	41	82.00	36	72.00	26	52.00	22	44.00	37	74.00
Haveri	41	82.00	0	0.00	0	0.00	43	86.00	36	72.00	28	56.00	26	52.00	38	76.00
Uttar Kannada	42	84.00	0	0.00	0	0.00	37	74.00	35	70.00	27	54.00	24	48.00	34	68.00
Total	308	88.00	1	0.29	0	0.00	284	81.14	229	65.43	173	49.43	159	45.43	273	78.00

Table 4.71 clearly shows that 308 out of 350 respondents expressed that the SHGs have expanded their business in the area under study. 284 respondents opined that there is an improvement in the assets of the SHGs, 273 responded that the living standard of the members of the SHGs have been increased to a considerable extent, 229 respondents asserted that there is an increase in income and savings, 173 said that their deposits with the banks has been raised and 159 agreed that SHGs have opened banks accounts and have deposited their own savings. The other two factors such as construction of new office buildings and store rooms, workshops etc., are insignificant in the study area.

Impact of Bank Loan on SHG's

Micro-finance programme enable the members to save, and setup and expand a credit fund consisting of savings and/or resources mobilized from donors/banks, so that members can initiate income-generating activities. It also enables the members to acquire assets. The impact of bank loan on SHGs in the study area is shown in the Table 4.72.

Table 4.72: Impact of Bank Loan on SHGs

Sl. No.	Impact	Improvement	
		Yes	No
1	2	3	4
1.	Investment in Fixed Assets has gone up	382	519
2.	Improvement in infrastructure *viz.*, lighting, storage, transport of members, etc.	276	625
3.	Working capital position has improved	144	757
4.	SHG members have reduced their dependence on money lenders	172	729
5.	SHG members have benefited in education of children, medical expenses, marriage expenditure, etc.	208	693
6.	Loans have helped in meeting marketing operations of SHG and members of SHG	307	594
7.	Improvement of Agriculture of Members	453	448
8.	Additional Milch Animals Purchased	407	494
9.	Overall Income of the Members has gone up	424	477
10.	Standard of living of members has gone up *viz.*		–

1	2	3	4
	1. Better Housing	58	843
	2. Use of Latrines	36	865
	3. Fans, Fridges	402	499
	4. Telephone, Mobile	896	005
	5. Economic Empowerment	508	393
	6. Political Empowerment	34	867
11.	Others	–	–

Table 4.72 indicates that the loan assistance provided by the banks and other agencies have a positive impact on the SHG's and its members. It has made a considerable impact on the life and economic and social activities of the members of the SHGs of the study area.

Conclusion

The financial assistance provided to the SHGs for the development of socio-economic status reached the economically marginalized and socially backward, in the study area. The SHG bank-linkage programme in the study area has been working in right direction in eradicating the poverty of the rural poor and in the empowerment of the women. Still there is a vast scope for micro-entrepreneurial activities in the rural as well as urban areas. Women share in rural employment in the study areas has increased significantly; it is still much lower as compared to other areas. Therefore, more and more SHGs should be encouraged so that they provide development funds to the neglected target groups which in turn lead to socio-economic development of the region. The social impact of micro-finance through SHGs under study is discussed in the V chapter.

5

SOCIAL IMPACT OF MICRO-FINANCE

It has universally been accepted that micro-finance is a very effective tool for alleviating poverty. Micro-finance through SHGs create confidence in poor especially women who are mostly invisible in the social structure. SHGs play a significant role in transforming socio-economic and political conditions of the rural poor especially the women in India. Many studies have attempted to measure the impact of micro-finance in terms of income, employment and other socio-economic outcomes (Hulme and Mousely, 1996: Schuler and Hashemi, 1994).

Micro-financing through SHGs could benefit overall society by overcoming the liquidity. It generates benefits to only that portion of the poor, that is able to use loan for income-generating activities. Borrowing will increase their income and sustain self-employment. The post independence era in the country has seen a series of policy interventions for assuring on effective institutional arrangements for meeting the financial needs of the society. The Banks were nationalized, directed lending by way of insisting the financial institutions for lending to priority sectors, NABARD established poverty alleviation programmes were launched and economic reforms were introduced by the government to uplift and empower the rural poor especially the women. But, were not enough to tackle the problem of poverty and at the same time subsidy linked government programmes could not prove effective, because of the huge member households, limited resources, inadequacies in the implementation, huge implementation cost, leakages etc. The NABARD's experiment proved successful as the poor people could successfully access credit from formal credit system. This paved way for launching of pilot projects of forming 255 SHGs and credit linking them with banks. The implementation of the pilot project was an instant success. Southern states including Karnataka were in the forefront. This, SHG Bank-Linkage Programme has been the most successful poverty alleviation programme so far. More them 69 Lakh SHG were linked to Bank by the end of March 2010. This clearly shows that the poor especially women in India particularly in Karnataka are benefited by this programme. All these developments have made a social and cultural impact on the members of the SHGs.

CHANGE IN SOCIO-ECONOMIC CONDITIONS

Financial linkage has made a tremendous change in the socio-economic conditions of the households. The income source of SHG members has been increased to manifolds, their living standard has been raised and the households using more number of assets than earlier. The direct access to credit has given them new status for beginning of long-term improvement in the family.

The improved economic status has made them to provide better education and health to their children. The social status in the village as well as at home has been significantly improved. They are now taking active part in family decisions. Same of the members spent their earnings directly without seeking permission. Family members have changed outlook towards women. Some of the women become the members of school betterment and advisory committee and members of village panchayat. There is considerable reduction of dependence on money lenders. The participation of women in SHG activities results in coming into contact with banks, co-operatives, rural-co-operative societies, trusts and also helps them to interact with private service providers. This is expected to result in gaining functional literacy and develop leadership qualities. In this background an attempt has been made in this chapter is to examine the social benefits accruing to the members of the SHGs under study.

SOCIAL IMPACT OF SHGS

The SHG movement in the area under study has a considerable impact on the social life of the members. Access of SHG members to credit enabled them to undertake diversifies the occupational pattern. Before joining the group the households used to put their small savings in single occupational activity. Credit access benefited the households to acquire productive assets. The raise in income has resulted in social transformation to a considerable extent in the study area. Though, social impact of the groups is not quantifiable, on the basis of the responses collected from the respondents on particular point, conclusions are drawn.

Table 5.1: Social Impact on Members of the SHGs

Sl. No.	Social Impact	No. of Respondents	Per cent
1.	Participation in family decision	583	64.71
2.	Social status in the village	064	07.10
3.	Mobility, Functional Literacy	597	66.26
4.	Knowledge and information	631	70.03
5.	Self-confidence and courage	369	40.95
6.	Participation of social activities	237	26.30
7.	Admit of children into the school	489	54.27
8.	Health awareness	463	51.39

Source: Field Survey.

PARTICIPATION IN FAMILY DECISIONS

Participation in family decisions is a major factor that through light on the performance of the SHG members. Usually, the member's are taking part in two types of decisions *i.e.,* purchases made for the household, for children and for herself. This includes purchase of utensils, cloths for children, sari and provision etc. The other decisions in which member's are participating relating to production activities. These include purchase and sale of assets, repair, renovation of house, purchase of milch animals, leasing and other assets.

583 out of 901 respondents expressed that they are activity participated in the family decisions. They have a say in the family

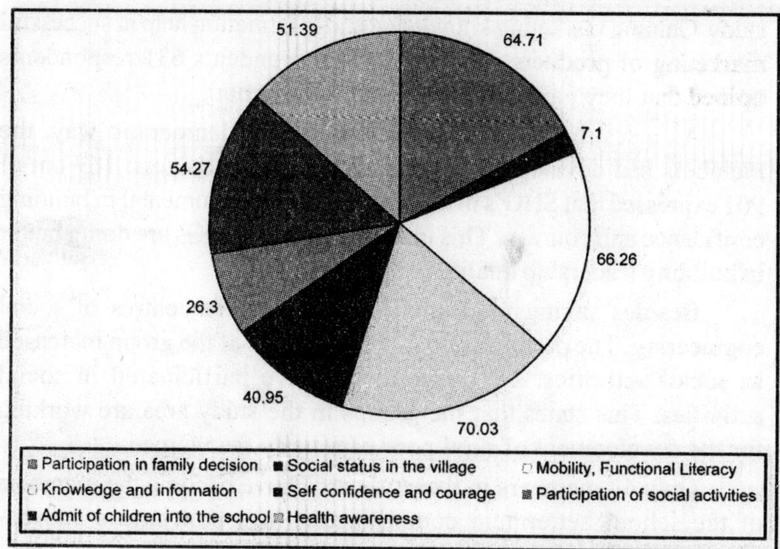

Fig. 5.1: Social Impact on Members of the SHGs

decisions. This clearly shows that economic development in members; definitely enabled the members of the group to take active part in family decisions.

The mobility of the members helps in acquiring communication skills. They visit more frequently to banks, co-operative societies and other private organizations and are attending meetings called by the groups. This has resulted in gaining banking and marketing knowledge. 597 out 901 respondents expressed that participation in SHG activities enabled them to attain functional literacy. Before joining the SHGs, they never visited the banks. Now they are approaching the banks on rotation basis. The interaction with the bankers has made them to learn many things.

SHG's in the area under study can be a platform to discuss, develop and establish positive attitudes regarding various issues concerned to members and the group. Participation in meetings, discussions and programmes assist the members to acquaint knowledge and information about these issues which they do not find solution without proper knowledge and information. Marketing of products of SHG is one of the major problems of the SHG's under study. Gaining marketing knowledge and information help in successful marketing of products. Out of 901 of respondents 631 respondents opined that they gain knowledge and information.

As a result of SHG's functioning in a democratic way, the members had developed self-confidence and awareness. 369 out of 901 expressed that SHG's in the study area are instrumental in building confidence and courage. This indicates that the SHGs are doing better in building leadership quality in members.

Besides savings and credit the groups are centres of social engineering. The participation of the members of the group increased in social activities. 237 respondents have participated in social activities. This states that the groups in the study area are working for the development of rural poor especially the women.

Only 64 members in the study area have become the members of the school betterment committee, village panchayats and co-operative societies.

The 73rd Constitutional Amendment to the Panchayat Raj Act (Passed in 1992) gave 33 per cent reservations to women in panchayats, have intensified the need for political reservation. SHG's are doing their best in preparing the members to involve in politics.

Some of the members in the study area are involved in community services and their wordings are being given importance while taking community decisions.

Members of the SHGs especially women were co-opted with little power respect or political status.

Members are taking active part in all the elections and also contested in village election and few of them have been won in the elections.

Admit of Children in to the Social

The perception towards education has changed significantly after association with SHGs. Majority of the respondents expressed that they are sending their children to school continuously. The drop-out of boys and girl student has come down in the study area. 489 respondents out of 901 agreed that they are admitting their children to the school. Majority of the respondents felt that school education would help in obtaining employment, awareness and literacy.

Moreover, members expressed that their children should not suffer like them due to lack of education. This is a major positive change in the perception of poor households in the area under study.

Health Awareness

The respondents after joining the SHGs possess health awareness in the study area. Respondents are spending more on medical care of their children. 463 respondents agreed that they are consulting the doctors immediately when their children fall sick. They also have awareness about family planning and economic benefits of a small family. The participation in SHG activities enabled the household's awareness about child marriage, dowry, status of widow and pre-mature killing of girl child etc. These developments have made a social transformation of the members of the SHGs under study.

Self-confidence

Self-confidence refers to the realisation of their identity potentiality and power to perform the activity. However this is absent in real situation especially in rural areas. Involvement of people in income generation activities builds self-confidence in members of the group. This helped them to face and react to the problems. Out of 901 respondents 497 opined that they have confidence in themselves and are ready to face the real life situations.

It implies the peaceful co-existence of people from different background and social groups. In the study area, some groups are single caste and some are mixed caste groups. All these groups overcome social, cultural and religious barriers to achieve equality.

Before Joining SHGs

1. Opposition from the family members for SHG formation.
2. Women had no respect in the society.
3. Women are not treated on equal footings with men.
4. Women had no exposure.
5. Women were treated as slaves.
6. Women have no independence and the men never encouraged to act independently.
7. Women were excluded from decision-making.

8. Parents/husband never allow women to attend meetings and they do not assist in household activities.
9. Comments from the society for their SHG activities.
10. Women were controlled by the parents before marriage and by husband after marriage.
11. Women were discouraged with regards to education.
12. Women were not allowed to go outside. Even if they were allowed, they were being told to return home within six PM.
13. Since women were working within the four walls, they lack knowledge about the outside world.
14. There is a greater disparity between men and women, and uneducated and educated women.

After Joining SHGs

1. Women were found with self-confidence.
2. Women were given respect in the village and community.
3. Women have a say in the family.
4. Women mobilization increased to a considerable extent.
5. Some of the women members of the group have become members of the school betterment committee, village panchayats and taluka panchayats.
6. Women are actively taking part in family decisions.
7. Women have a greater control over their earnings.
8. Women never depend on their family members in marketing.
9. Women are spending more on education and health of their children.
10. Women were actively involved in SHG activities and are encouraged to attend meetings.
11. Men have realised that group activity will fetch extra income.
12. Women were economically developed and have become independent.
13. Men are supporting for group activity.
14. Women have attained functional literacy.

Conclusion

The association of members with the SHGs has made a social transformation in the area under study. The members' role is immense in the family as well as community decisions. They are spending more on education and health of their children and family members. They are admitting their children into the schools and have health consciousness. Some of the members have won the Panchayat elections. The attitude towards themselves and others has been changed. But, the rate of change is not enough and hence more and more SHGs are to be established in this area to involve the rural poor in to the mainstream.

6 FINDINGS AND SUGGESTIONS

Credit plays a crucial role in economic empowerment of the poor and the disadvantaged. Provision of credit under various alleviation programmes have been taken up since independence from time to time. Still, a large section of the population in India lives below poverty line. Delivering adequate, timely, credit to poor is the only weapon to counteract this state of affairs. UN in its Economic and Social Council Meet on July 25, 1997 was stressed the role of micro-credit in eradication of poverty. India has been experiencing micro-credit in the form of Self-Help Groups (SHGs) as a part of formal credit delivery system. Government of India has taken up many steps for the linkage of SHGs with formal financial institutions. SHG bank-linkage programme aimed at providing a cost effective mechanism for providing financial services to the unreached poor. So far micro-finance is concerned, the women are found to be the greatest beneficiaries. SHGs were a pilot programme in the beginning. Today, SHGs are fast reshaping the lower strata of the society. The physical and financial outreach of the programme has been impressive in as much as there are more than 69 lakh savings linked SHGs and more than 49 lakh credit linked SHGs on 31-March, 2010, covering 970 lakh poor households with a credit flow of over Rs. 28038.28 crore.

This shows that the programme has been successful not only in meeting the credit needs of the poor, but also in strengthening collective self-help capacities of the poor at the local level, leading to their empowerment. Against this background an attempt has been made to assess the performance of the SHGs in transforming socio-economic life of the poor in the Mumbai Karnataka Region.

Micro-credit programme to the poor and the under privileged people has widely recognised a key strategy all over the world and also in India. Micro-credit programme in India is distinctly different from poverty alleviation programmes targeting the rural and urban households with emphasis on women borrowers. Despite the vast network of bank branches, a large segment of the rural poor depend on non-institutional financial sources for their credit needs. Micro-finance is expected to play pivotal role in poverty alleviation and employment generation in India and also in the study area.

Mumbai Karnataka Region a backward area in the state of Karnataka and agriculture becomes the main occupation of the people. Majority of the population stays in rural areas and more poverty prevails in the rural side. Though the region has a huge bank network, the existing network is insufficient to meet the requirements. There is a gap between the demand and the supply. Studies reveal that rural credit has come down. The SHG bank-linkage programme and SGSY scheme were accelerated in recent years. This has a considerable impact on the SHG members of this area. Hence, the need was arise to study the socio-economic impact micro-financing through SHGs in the study area with the following objectives.

Objectives

The principal objectives of the study are:

1. To study the impact of SHGs Bank-linkage programme on socio-economic status of the members of the group.
2. To study whether the SHGs are instrumental in enhancing economic and social status of the members.
3. To study the extent of mobilization of funds and generation of income by the SHGs.
4. To ascertain the problems before SHGs.
5. To offer suggestions to overcome the problems before SHGs.

FINDINGS OF THE STUDY

To fulfill the objectives of the study, the information and data have been collected from various sources. After careful observation of the data, suggestions are made as per the findings of the research. The main findings of the study are as follows:

Economic Impacts

Socio-economic Characteristics of the Members of the SHG:

- More than 95 per cent of the SHG members in the study area are female.
- The members between the age group of 21-50 years are more prone to joining SHG and even out of these the major portion of the members belong to the age group of 31-40 years in the area under study.
- It is evident from the study that, 58.55 per cent of the SHG members of the study area are illiterates, 8.44 per cent members have an education up to primary level and 29.76 per cent are educated up to secondary level.
- 57.71 per cent SHG members of the study area belong to BPL category.
- Table 4.7 shows that 38.15 per cent of the SHG members belong to labour class, while 26.52 per cent from business category and 16.96 per cent belong to agriculture group.
- 57.30 per cent of the SHG members of the study area earn between Rs. 10,000 - 20,000 and 37.60 per cent earn below Rs. 10,000. This indicates that majority of the respondents fall in to a low income group.

Capital Resources

- It is observed from the Table 4.9 that capital was collected by various sources. The major sources of capital are savings and bank loan.

Investment of the SHG's

- Internal lending and bank deposits are the two prominent areas of investment of SHG's of the areas under study.

Savings internal lending of the SHG's

- The total average savings of the SHGs registered at Rs. 50832.47. The mean own collection of the SHGs under study was found to be Rs. 57797.03 and the average loan from the bank amounted to Rs. 175565.50.

Purpose for which Loan in given

- Loans are provided by the SHG's for different purposes in the study area. Table 4.12 shows that in all the districts of the study area majority of the SHG's provide loan for agriculture and business.

Bank Operations

- The average total deposits of the SHG's with the bank amounts to Rs. 46976.4 and the mean borrowings are Rs. 153939.8.
- The main purposes of borrowings of SHG's in the study area are trade, agriculture and dairying.
- It is evident from the Table that 65.59 per cent of the respondents in the area under study opined that the banks are providing loans to the extent requested by the SHG's.
- The average percentage of loan obtained in relation to the amount applied was 68.77.
- The majority of banks in the area under study fix-up maximum limit of loan to SHGs for different purposes.
- Table 4.18 indicates that, 65.59 per cent of the SHGs respond that they are getting adequate loan from the banks.
- 69.59 per cent of the SHGs expressed that the banks are providing additional loan before the earlier loan is repaid.

Nature of Security, Time Taken by the Banks and Bank Procedures

- Majority of the banks in the study area insist guarantees of NGOs, bank deposits and buildings as securities.
- The average time taken by the banks in releasing the loans to SHGs varies between 2.45 to 3.36 days.
- Majority of the SHGs in the study area are of the opinion that the bank procedure is simple.
- It is evident from the Table 4.23 that 86.79 per cent of the SHGs do not get interest subsidy.
- 96.00 per cent of the SHGs do not receive the subsidy amount promptly.

- 90.12 per cent of the SHGs under study do not pass the subsidy benefits to member borrowers.

Utilisation and Impact of Bank Loan

- 72.70 per cent of the SHGs expressed that they have utilised all the amount of loan obtained from the bank.
- In all the districts of the study area, except Belagum district, more BPL members have availed loan.
- 68.92 per cent of the members of the SHGs availed loan for the first time in the study area.
- The mean number of members taken repeat finance was 13.33.

Impact of Bank Loan on SHG

- It is evident from the Table 4.30 and 4.31 that the bank loan has made a positive economic impact on the members of the SHGs in the area under study. It is observed that, 94.12 per cent respondents respond that the standard of living of the members has gone-up. 89.23 per cent opined that the loan helped in meeting the marketing operations and 88.46 per cent members said an improvement in agriculture. 85.24 per cent members benefited in education, health and others and 82.46 per cent said that their income has been increased.

Repayment of Loan by SHG

- The Table 4.34 clearly shows that the banks of the study area usually fix 30-36 monthly repayment installments for loans.
- 93.45 per cent of the SHGs in the area under study agree that the loan installments are convenient.
- 68.15 per cent of the SHGs do not get relief from the bank on request for inconveniences of loan installments.
- The major inconveniences to the SHGs under study with regard loan installments are; more interest cost, members are not prompt and hence SHGs find it difficult to keep up the schedule, income of the SHG is not growing fast, subsidy not released in time and rigid bank policies.

Bank General Information

- On average the banks in the study area have two officers, one accountant, 3 clerks and 2-3 other staff.

- The mean number of SHG account in a bank was 100.6, the mean savings amount was found to be Rs. 370591.2. The average number of SHGs financed by the banks registered at 23.9, the average amount financed was Rs. 18888390.0 and the average loan amount outstanding accounts to Rs. 1655088.6.

Loans to SHGs

- 66.00 per cent of the banks issue loans directly to SHGs in the study area, 28.57 per cent of the banks disburse loan both by directly and through NGOs and 5.43 per cent issue through NGOs.
- The determination of the amount of loan largely based on amount of deposits, guidelines of the bank head office and need of the loan amount of the SHGs.
- It is evident from the Table 4.43 that small trade, dairying, small enterprise and farm operations are the main purposes of loans to SHGs by the bank in the study area.

Loan Accounts

- The mean number of loan accounts of women is more than the mean number of loan accounts of men.
- The average total loan amount of men is more than the average loan amount of women.
- The main purposes of providing loan to SHGs in the study area are dairying, small trade, small enterprises, and consumption and farm operations.
- The ratio of the total loan amount to SHGs and total loan from the banks was found to be Rs. 1332863.9 lakh.

Interest on Loans to SHGs

- The average rate of interest charged on loans to SHGs by the banks in the study area was 7.91.
- 92.29 per cent of the banks under study not charge different rate of interest for different type of loans to SHGs.
- Almost all the banks in the study area demand ration card, photo of the members and certificates while releasing the loan to SHGs.

- The mean repeat loan has been shows on increasing trend during the year 2005-06 to 2008-09.
- Banks in the study area usually take two weeks time in releasing loan after receiving the application. 56.57 per cent banks will take two weeks, 32.29 per cent will take one week.
- Banks do not fix maximum limit of loan for different purposes of SHGs in the study area.
- Some of the bank branches fix maximum limit of loan for small enterprise and small trade.
- 98.86 per cent of the banks fix target of loan finance to SHGs every year.

Pre-Sanction Measures

- Obtaining the project details, making on the spot study of the project, study of the financial sources of the SHGs and study of the surety's financial soundless are the major steps taken by the banks while estimating the credit worthiness and credit needs of the borrower.
- Fewer applications for loan, lower amount applied by SHGs than the target kept and others factors responsible for falling short of the target amount in the study area.
- 56.57 per cent of the banks in the study area are not interested in knowing the SHGs involvement in other loans.
- It is observed from the Table 4.62 that, 89.71 per cent of the banks in the study area assess the repayment capacity of the SHGs.

Utilisation of Loan by the SHGs

- More than 45 per cent of the banks enforce the proper utilisation of the loans by the SHGs.
- 98.86 per cent of the banks in the area under study release the next loan only after first loan are properly utilised.
- The instance of miss-utilisation is hardly 10.29 per cent in the study area.
- 44.9 per cent of the banks expressed that less than 2 per cent of loans diverted or miss-utilised and 29.4 per cent opined that, the loan mis-utilisation per centage was 2 to 5. Loan miss-

utilisation to the extent of 5 to 8 per cent was found to be 8.9 per cent.

- Men SHGs in the area under study have diverted the bank loan.
- 84.00 per cent of the banks go for periodical inspection of SHGs.
- In SGSY and SJSRY government sponsored schemes the incidence of miss-utilisation was more pronounced.

Recover of Loan from the SHGs

- The mean number of installments of loan repayment was 35.51.
- Bank head office, guidelines of the NABARD/RBI and bank manager are the persons fixing the installments.
- 86.29 per cent of banks in the study area do not fix different number of installments for loans to different categories.
- The repayment of loans by SHGs in the area under study is prompt and satisfactory only 10.57 per cent of the SHGs have delayed in the repayment of loan.
- Sending reminders, telephone reminders, issuing notices are the major steps taken by the banks for recovery of loans from SHGs.

Training of SHGs

- Around 80 per cent of the banks are not involved in the training of SHGs.
- 94.86 per cent of the banks opined that training is necessary activity before financing SHGs in the study area.
- It is evident from the bank finance to SHGs impacted positively in the study area. SHGs have expanded their business and have increased their assets. The members of the SHGs have improved their income and their living standards and increased their savings and bank deposits.

Social Impacts

- The members of the group especially women in the study area have a say in the family decisions.
- The women members took part in community decisions.
- Status of the members in the village has been significantly improved.

- The association with SHGs enabled the members to acquire functional literacy.
- There is a rise of self-confidence, courage in member of the study area.
- Women admitted their children to higher studies by taking loan from the group.

Others

- It is observed from the study that the spread of the SHGs shall be slow where the livelihood opportunities are limited in the study area.
- It is found from the study that the spread of SHGs is found to be low in Bagalkot, Belgaum, Bijapur and Haveri districts. The spread of SHGs is Moderate in Gadag district and good in Dharwad and Uttar Kannada districts in the area under study.

Problems faced by the Respondents

- Lack of time to participate in all the activities of the SHGs.
- Timely non-availability of financial help.
- The amount of loan is too small to take up a viable business.
- No support for starting a new activity.
- The respondents faced with the problem of marketing products produced by the SHGs.
- Political Interference in increasing the number of SHGs.
- Variable rate of interest.
- Lack of adequate training facilities.
- Lack of field exposure.

SUGGESTIONS

In the light of the findings emerged from the study, the following suggestions have been made for the growth and development of SHG movement in Mumbai Karnataka Region.

1. *Education Improvement*: Around 59 per cent of the SHG members in the area under study are illiterate and 8.55 per cent members have an education up to primary level. Therefore they should be given education by establishing informal education centres in all the districts at the block level for providing basic

education as well as continuing of education. SHGs have to take up a campaign to impact functional literacy to their members and NGOs in this area, have to work for the improvement of literacy.

2. *Access to Credit*: It was found from the study that 51.71 per cent of the members of the SHGs belong to BPL category and 37.66 per cent members earn annually below Rs. 10,000. This clearly indicates that most of the members of the group hail from poor families. Despite, the vast network of bank branches in the study area, poor are unable to access formal credit. They need credit to meet social obligations and to imitate small income generating activities and to buy agricultural inputs. Hence, accelerating micro-finance programme in this area do provide access to credit for the poor, enable them to undertake income-generating activities. This will lead to gradual improvement in the quality of their life and builds self-confidence in members.

3. *Adequate and Timely Supply of Credit*: Micro-credit loans are too small to make a dent in poverty alleviation and growth. Therefore, it should be raised and the loan products should suit client's needs. The determination of the loans in the area under study is largely depends on the amount of deposits kept in the bank. Since, the SHGs under study have low bank deposits; they do not get big loans. The amount sanctioned is often inadequate for economic viability of the group members. Especially, the new SHGs do not get better loans, so, they do not involve in income-generating activities.

4. *Increase Savings*: The saving not only inculcates the habit of thrift but also helps in developing confidence in members of the SHGs. Hence, the saving habit must be encouraged as a value in itself and not just as a means of increasing the fund position of the group. It also controls unnecessary consumption.

It was found from the study that the average savings of the SHGs was Rs. 50,837.49. This is merge amount, which is used in internal lending by the SHGs of the area under study. Therefore, the amount of savings should be increased by proper encouragement to members so that, larger amount can be available for internal leading.

5. *Production Loan Should be Encouraged*: Members of the SHGs use micro-credit not only for income-generation, but also for consumption needs. The purpose wise break-up of current loans of groups reveals that trade; agriculture and dairying are the prominent purposes for which money was borrowed and the other purposes are micro enterprises consumption and others. The mean borrowings were found to be Rs. 1, 53,939.8. It is clear from the fact that the members of the SHGs in the area under study have utilised major portion of the borrowings for income-generation activity. Some portion was used for consumption needs like education and health etc. In future, production loan should be encouraged, entrepreneurship development programme (EDP), capacity building and skill up gradation activities can be promoted among the members which enables them to utilise more amount of loan in income-generation activities.
6. *Nature of Security:* The banks insist various types of securities such as guarantee of NGOs, bank deposits and buildings while sanctioning loans to SHGs. Therefore, there is a need to activate the NGOs in rural area to participate in the effective implementation of the programme. Bank approach towards NGOs should be positive. Bank deposit has to be increased by inculcating among the members the habit of thrift. Very less number of SHGs has their own buildings and hence, building security is insignificant in the area under study.
7. *Scheme Specific Incentive*: One of the major findings of the study was, 86.79 per cent of the SHGs do not get interest subsidy and 96 per cent of the SHGs of the study area do not receive the subsidy amount promptly and 90.12 per cent of the SHGs under study do not pass subsidy benefits to member borrowers. This has caused a feeling in members that they are neglected. Another observation of the study is that the members prefer subsidy schemes rather than non-subsidy schemes. The SGSY is a micro enterprise scheme with subsidy and SHG-NABARD linkage scheme is non-subsidy scheme. Hence, conflict among the members arises when some groups are sanctioned subsidy and some are not. Therefore, instead scheme specific incentive based

on past performance could be permitted. Proper policy initiatives from the government in this regard are needed.

8. *Strengthening the Existing Groups*: The micro-credit provided to the SHGs members in the selected districts of the area under study made a positive social and economic impact. Their living standard has been increased, income of the members has gone-up, their expenditure pattern has changed, and social status has been increased and is benefited in education, health and other areas. This impact of micro-credit on the group members in the study area is only moderate. Hence, all efforts should be concentrated on strengthening the existing groups further.

9. *Repayment of Loan*: The major finding with regards to the repayment of loan by the SHGs was inconveniences in repayment of loans. More interest cost, income of SHG was not growing fast, subsidy not realised in time, rigid bank policies and the members of the SHG are not prompt and hence SHGs find it difficult to keep up the schedule are some of the reasons for irregularities in the repayment of loans by the SHGs in the study area. Therefore, transformation of the repayment culture is required. Bankers must change their attitude towards small loans to the poor-people including women as a social obligation of treating them as potential business entrepreneurs. Some policies in this regard are initiated.

10. *Importance to Men SHGs*: At present micro-finance programmes are popular only among the women in India and also in the study area. It was found from the study that more than 95 per cent of the SHG members are female and the average number of loan accounts of women is more than the average number of loan account of men. Hence, men and youth groups should also be promoted.

11. *Short of Target Amount:* It was found from the study that, though, banks are keeping the target number and amount very every year, most of the banks fail in reaching the target number and amount due to, fewer applications and lower amount applied for loan. Therefore, SHGs in the study area are to be linked properly with the banks and awareness is to be created among the members of the SHGs.

12. *Incidence of Miss-utilisation:* The incidence of miss-utilisation of loan in SGSY and SJSRY programmes is more pronounced in the area under study. This can be minimized and controlled with proper polices by the government.
13. *Training*: Majority of the banks were not involved in the training of SHGs and around 95 per cent of the banks intended that training is a necessary activity before financing SHGs in the area under study. Hence, there is need to take steps in the training of SHG members and conduct skill development activities at the block level to make the micro-financing more meaningful. Periodical time to time training helps the SHG members' deep involvement in the programme. EDPs and work related training courses should be organized for the benefit of members. Members should be trained in specific areas such as decision-making, account, keeping, communication skills and management without imposing financial burden on them. Training should be supported by extension service and adequate supply of imports even after completion of the training.
14. *Social Impacts*: Micro-financing through SHGs has made a social impact on the members in the study area. But this impact seems to be moderate because, the members especially women facing number of challenges in the present society. Therefore, clustering of SHGs may have a strong social potential.
15. *Books Keeping*: Account keeping at the group level has emerged as a very weak aspect of SHG functioning, Hence importance is to be given to financial literacy and communication. User friendly and simple records need to be designed.
16. *Women Exposure to Outside World*: Women in rural areas lack exposure to outside world. Hence, SHGs programmes should be designed to make them participate actively in all the activities related to socio-economic transformation.
17. *SHG Number:* SHG growth seems to be supply driven approach of pushing external loans on SHGs. Therefore, amount and timings of such loans should depend on member capacities, not on target.

General Suggestions

18. *Awareness about the Schemes*: Some of the SHG beneficiaries in the study area had no clear idea about thrift and loans. Awareness is to be created with regard to schemes and their process. Awareness is also to be created with regards to education, health etc.
19. *Repeat Loans*: 68.92 per cent of the members of the SHGs availed loan for the first time in the study area and the amount of loan were too small and hence not economically viable. Repeated borrowing or booster dose is no doubt helping the members to invest the funds in income-generation activities.
20. *Assistance to Micro-Entrepreneurs:* SHGs in the study area should strengthen economic base of their members by identifying and arising micro entrepreneurs within the group.
21. *Self-Employment Opportunities*: SHGs should be allowed to peruse the self-employment opportunities on individual basis and must be encouraged to undertake group enterprises.
22. *More Attention to SGSY Scheme*: More attention is required under SGSY for promotion of non-form activities and for which appropriate technology and institutional support needs to be strengthened.
23. *Provision of Marketing for the SHG Products:* There should be more budgetary allocation on market development in order to provide an effective platform for marketing of SHG products.
24. *Middlemen Interference*: Middlemen interference between SHGs and the bank should be avoided. Government should make necessary policy to avoid too much interference between SHGs and the bank.
25. *Planned Interventions of Technology and Credit*: SHG is an import vehicle for social development of the households. But the present social development is nominal. Hence, to attain good social status in the society planned interventions of technology and credit are necessary.
26. *Indifferent Attitude of Banks*: Some bankers show in some cases indifferent attitude in promoting SHGs in the study area. Therefore, necessary steps should be taken to change the attitude with regards to strengthening of the SHGs.

27. *Political Interference:* Due to political interference the number of SHGs has been increased. The groups should be formed on the basis of need but not on the basis of political motivation.
28. *Field Exposures*: Field exposure visit to group members may be organized so that they can get themselves exposed to other groups and will get an opportunity to learn from others.
29. *Backward and Forward of Linkages*: The SHGs have to invest money in income-generating activities for their sustenance and improvement in their standard of living. However, rural households in the reign are not able to get opportunities for investment in promising enterprises. Therefore there need to assist them by giving backward and forward linkages.
30. *More Focus on Low Spread Areas*: The spread of SHGs is not even in Karnataka, The spread has been observed to be low in four districts such as: *(i)* Bagalkot, *(ii)* Bijapur, *(iii)* Belgaum and *(iv)* Haveri districts in the Study area. The spread of SHGs is moderate in Gadag and the spread of SHGs is good in Dharwad and Uttara Kannada districts. Hence the promoters of SHGs have to focus more on districts where the spread so far has been either low or moderate to minimize the imbalance.

Conclusion

The financial assistance provided to the SHGs for the development of socio-economic status reached the economically marginalized and socially backward in the area under study. The SHG bank-linkage programme in the study area has working in the right direction in alleviating the poverty of the rural poor and in the empowerment of women. Still there is a vast scope for micro-entrepreneurial activities in the rural as well as urban areas. Women share in rural employment in the study area has increased significantly; it is still much lower as compared to other areas. Therefore, more and more SHGs should be encouraged so that they provide development funds to the neglected target groups which in turn lead to socio-economic development of the region.

BIBLIOGRAPHY

A. Karunaithal (2009), Linkage between SHGs and Banks in India; Banking, Micro-finance and SHGs in India; New Century Publications, New Delhi, p. 165,166.

A. P. Samal (2008), Dynamics of Micro-finance and Social Transformation; Micro-finance and Rural Development in India; New Century Publications, New Delhi, India, p. 84.

Ambika Prasad Pati (2010), Financial Sustainability of Micro-financing; Gyan Publishing House, New Delhi, p. 73.

Awadesh Kumar Singh (2008), Empowering Rural Women through Micro-financing; Serials Publications, New Delhi.

Ayub Khan Dawood (2009), Micro-finance and Rural Development; Banking, Micro-finance and SHGs in India; New Century Publications, New Delhi, p. 174.

B. N. Rath (2011), Livelihood and Micro-finance, Navayug Books International, Delhi.

B. N. Rath (2011), Micro-finance and Risk Management, Navayug Books International Delhi.

Basu, *et al.* (2002), Empowerment of Women in the Context of Development – Some Issues and Suggestions; *Journal of the Indian Anthropological Society*, 37(3), pp. 209-221, November.

Bhuvan I. B. (2007), Performance of Micro-finance Providers in Karnataka; Dissertation; University of Agricultural Sciences, Dharwad.

Christabella P. J. (2009), Women Empowerment through Capacity Building – The Role of Micro-finance; Concept Publishing Company, New Delhi.

D. Sunder Ram (2009), Women Empowerment in Political Institutions: An Indian Perspective; Kanishka Publishers and Distributors, New Delhi.

Debadatta K. Panda (2010), Understanding Micro-finance; Willy India Pvt. Ltd., New Delhi, India.

Debnarayan Sarkar (2008), Indian Micro-finance: Lessons from Bangladesh; Economic and Political Weekly, Vol. 43, No. 01, January 5-11, pp. 18-20.

Deepali Pant Joshi (2010), Micro-finance for Micro Change: Emerging Challenges; Gyan Publishing House, New Delhi.

Devendra Prasad Pandey (2009), Micro-finance Management; Adhyayan Publishers and Distributors, New Delhi.

Dr. M. Edwin Gnanadhas (2011), Micro-finance and Self-Help Groups, Discovery Publishing House Pvt. Ltd., New Delhi.

Dr. N. Lalitha (2003), Mainstreaming Micro-finance; Mohit Publications, New Delhi.

Dr. Rais Ahmed (2009), Micro-finance and Women Empowerment; Vol. 1, 2 and 3, Mittal Publications, New Delhi.

Dr. Sr. Rosa K. D. (2010), Empowerment of Women the Impact of Employment; Abhijit Publications, New Delhi.

Dr. Sudhansu Sekhar Nayak and Dr. Anilkumar Sahu (2011), Self-Help Groups and Micro-credit Institutions, Discovery Publishing House Pvt. Ltd., New Delhi.

Dr. Tanuj Kumar Bisoyi (2010), Rural Credit, Regional Rural Banks and Micro-finance; Abhijit Publications, New Delhi.

E. A. Narayana, E. V. Laxmi (2011), Women Development in India; Regal Publications, New Delhi.

Frances Sinha (2009), Micro-finance and Self-Help Groups in India; Practical Action Publishing, United Kingdom.

Gautam Kanwar, R. Kartikeya, Rajat Kapur and Rajat K. Baisya (2008), Micro-finance in the Indian Scenario: A Study on the Existing Models; *Indian Journal of Commerce*, Vol. 61, No. 3, July-September, 2008.

Gupta S. K. (2002), Formation and Functioning of SHGs in Hoshangabad District of Madhya Pradesh. *Land Bank Journal,* Vol. 41(1), pp. 25-31, June.

H. S. Shylendra (1998), Promoting Women's SHG – Lessons from an Action Research Project of IRMA, Gujarat.

H.S. Shylendra (2007), Micro-finance Bill: Missing the Forest for the Trees; *Economic and Political Weekly,* Vol. 42, No. 28, July 14-20, p. 2910.

Isher Judge Ahluwalia, I. M. D. Little (2010), India's Economic Reforms and Development – Essays for Manmohan Singh; Oxford University Press, New Delhi.

Jairam Ramesh (2007), SHG Revolution: What Next; *Economic and Political Weekly*, Vol. 42, No. 36, September 8-14, p. 3621.

Jaspreet Kaur Soni (2008), Women Empowerment – The Sustainable Challenges; Authors Press Global Network, Delhi, India.

Jayasheela, Shri Prasad H., Dinesh P. T. (2009), Micro-finance in India: A Tool for Women Empowerment; Serials Pubications, New Delhi, pp. 89-91.

Jayasheela, Shri Prasad H., Dinesh P. T. (2009), Micro-finance in India: A Tool for Women Empowerment; Serials Publications, New Delhi, pp. 143-144.

Jayasheelan Natarajan (2010), Micro-credit to Micro-enterprises; Dominant Publishers, New Delhi.

Jyothy (2002), SHGs under the Women's Development Programmes in Tamil Nadu. Achievements, Bottlenecks and Recommendations, Social Change, Vol. 32(3 and 4), pp. 195-204, September-December.

Kanak Kanti Bagachi (2009), Micro-finance and Rural Development a Critical Review; Abhijit Publications, New Delhi.

Karmakar K. G. (1998), SHI in Orissa – Some Conceptual Issues; Prajnana, 26(2), pp. 123-131.

Karunaithal (2009), Linkage between SHGs and Banks in India; Banking, Micro-finance and SHGs in India; New Century Publications, New Delhi, India, pp. 162-163 and 166.

Krishna Gupta (2010), Empowerment of Women: Emerging Dimensions; S. Chand and Company Ltd., New Delhi.

Laxmi P. Archana Gupta (2001), Self-Help Groups Innovations in Financing the Poor; Kurukshetra, Vol. 4, pp. 26-29.

M. Ramanjaneyalu (2006), Economic Empowerment of Women in India; Anmol Publications Pvt. Ltd., New Delhi.

M. P. Vasimalai, K. Narender (2007), Micro-finance Issues and Models; *Economic and Political Weekly*, Vol. 42, No. 13, March-31 to April-06, p. 1190.

M. R. Shollapur, Naveen K. Shetty (2011), Micro-finance and Sustainable Livelihood Promotions in India; Exel Books, New Delhi.

M. S. Gupta (2008), Micro-finance through SHGs: An Emerging Horizon for Rural Development; *Indian Journal of Commerce*, Vol. 61, No. 3, July-September, 2008.

M. S. Sriram, Radha Kumar (2007), Emergence of Micro-finance: Conditions in Which Micro-finance has Emerged in Certain Region; *Economic and Political Weekly,* Vol. 42, No. 49, December 8-14.

Mahir Shah, Ranga Rao, Vijayakumar (2007), Rural Credit in 20th Century India Overview of History and Perspectives; *Economic and Political Weekly*, Vol. 42, No. 15, April 14-20, p. 1351.

Malcom Harper (2007), What's Wrong with Micro-finance?; Practical Action Publishing, United Kingdom.

Manavinder Dilllon (2010), Economic Empowerment of Women; Holiday Book Store, Panchakula, (HR).

Mandakini Das, Pritirekha, Daspattanayak (2010), Empowering Women – Issues, Challenges and Strategies; Dominant Publishers and Distributors Pvt. Ltd., New Delhi.

Micro-finance Bill: One Step Forward or Two Step Backward; *Economic and Political Weekly*, Vol. 42, No. 12, March 24-30, 2008, p. 1006.

Mohammad Yunus (2004), Grameen Bank, Micro-Credit and Millennium Development Goals; *Economic and Political Weekly*, Vol. 49, No. 36, September 04-10, p. 4077.

Neeta Tapan (2010), Micro-credit, SHGs and Women Empowerment; New Century Publications, New Delhi, India, pp. 35-36.

P. Satish (2008), Misplaced Critique of Micro-finance Regulation Bill; *Economic and Political Weekly*, Vol. 43, No. 03, March 19-25, pp. 77-79.

P. Sindhuja (2011), Economic Empowerment of Women through Self-Help Groups; Discovery Publishing House Pvt. Ltd., New Delhi.

P. B. Rathod (2009), Women Development; ADB Publishers, Jaipur, India.

P. C. Dal (2008), Dynamics of Micro-finance and Social Transformation; Micro-finance and Rural Development in India; New Century Publications, New Delhi, India, p. 17.

Pankaj Gupta (2011), Studies in Economics of Micro-finance; Cyber Touch Publications, New Delhi.

Patil (2002), Rural Development Programme – A Study on Women Beneficiaries; *Indian Journal of Training and Development*, 32(4), pp. 89-90, October-December.

Pitta Usha (2010), Empowerment of Women and Self-Help Groups; Sonali Publications, New Delhi.

Prabhu Ghate (2007), Indian Micro-finance: The Challenges of Rapid Growth; Sage Publications, New Delhi.

Prasad C. (1995), Development of Women and Children in Rural Areas: Successful Case Studies. *Journal of Rural Development*, Vol. 14(1), pp. 65-87.

Priyanka Pandey (2009), Micro-Finance – A Review of International Experiences, Micro-finance and Women Empowerment (Patt-2), Mittal Publications, New Delhi, pp. 386-397.

Puyalvannan P. (2003), Micro-credit Innovations: A Study based on Micro-credit, Women Empowerment and Living of SHG with Co-operative Bankers in Tamil Nadu.

R. K. Sahoo (2008), Micro-finance, and the Empowerment of the Poor; Micro-finance and Rural Development in India; New Century Publications, New Delhi, India, p. 57.

R. N. Mishra, G. Chandrayya (2010), Micro-finance for Agriculture Development; Discovery Publishing House Pvt. Ltd., New Delhi.

Rajaram Dasgupta (2008), Micro-finance Legislation; *Economic and Political Weekly*, Vol. 43, No. 19, May 10-16, pp. 6-7.

Rajib Lochan Panigrahy, Sudhansu Sekhar (2010), Women Entrepreneurship; Discovery Publishing House Pvt. Ltd., New Delhi.

Rameshwari Pandya, Sarika Patel (2010), Women in the Un-organized Sector of India; New Century Publications, New Delhi.

S. Mahendra Dev (2011), Inclusive Growth in India; Oxford University Press, New Delhi.

S. Mahendra Dev, C. Ravi (2008), Rising Estimates of Poverty; *Economic and Political Weekly*, Vol. 43, No. 10, March 8-14, pp. 8-10.

S. Patra (2008), Micro-credit SHGs and Empowerment of Women; Micro-finance and Rural Development in India; New Century Publications, New Delhi, India, pp. 76-78.

S. K. Baral, S.C. Bihari (2010), Rural Marketing and Micro-finance; A.I.T.B.S. Publishers Delhi, India.

S. K. Das (2008), Micro-finance, SHGs and Poverty Removal; Micro-finance and Rural Development in India; New Century Publications, New Delhi, India, p. 65.

S. K. Das, B. P. Nanda (2008), Micro-finance and Sustainable Rural Development; Micro-finance and Rural Development in India; New Century Publications, New Delhi, India.

S. K. Das, B.P. Nanda, J. Rath (2008), Micro-finance and Rural Development in India; New Century Publications, New Delhi, India, Preface pp. 7-8.

Sangeeta Baradwaj Badal (2009), Gender, Social Structure and Women Empowerment – Status Report of Women in India; Rawat Publications, New Delhi.

Sarada Devi M. and Rayalu T. R. (2002), Factors Functioning in Women Empowerment in Urban Areas. *Journal of Community Guidance and Research*, Vol. 19(3), pp. 339-351, November.

Satpathy, Mishra, Ghadei (2009), Empowerment of Women: Perceptions and Realities; AGROBIOS (India), Jodhpur.

Satya Sundarum (2007), Micro-finance in India; B. R. Publishing Corporation, Delhi.

Shakun Palharya (2009), Micro-finance and Inclusive Growth in India; Micro-finance and Rural Development: A Critical Review; Abhijit Publications, New Delhi, pp. 45-46.

SHG Bank-Linkage in Karnataka, NABARD Report 2005-06.

SHG Bank-Linkage in Karnataka, NABARD Report 2006-07.

SHG Bank-Linkage in Karnataka, NABARD Report 2008-09.

SHG Bank-Linkage in Karnataka, NABARD Report 2009-10.

Singh A. (1995), NABARD – APARCA; International Seminar of Development of Rural Poor through the SHGs, May 29-30, Bangalore.

Sumanlata (2010), Towards Empowering Women – Views and Reviews; Akansha Publishing House, New Delhi.

Surendra K. Koushik, V. Rangarajan (2010), Micro-financing and Women's Empowerment; Serials Publications, New Delhi.

T. Lavanya (2010), Women Empowerment through Entrepreneurship; New Century Publications, New Delhi.

Tej Kumar Busoyi (2010), Micro-finance through SHGs: A Boost for Rural Women; Rural Credit, RRBs and Micro-finance, Abhijit Publications, New Delhi, p. 34.

Titus and Sebastin A.P. (2001), Impact of Micro-credit Programme of NGOs in Rural Women, IASSJ Quarterly, Vol. 20(2), pp. 135-142, October-December.

Tyagi B.P. (2011), Agriculture Economics and Rural Development; Jai Prakash Nath and Company, Meerut.

V. M. Rao (2004), Empowering Rural Women; Anmol Publications Pvt. Ltd., New Delhi.

Vijayakumar (2009), Banking, Micro-finance and SHGs in India; New Century Publications, New Delhi.

What do the New Poverty Estimates Imply; *Economic and Political Weekly*, Vol. 43, No. 43, October 25-31, 2008, pp. 31-44.

Women and Children Development Department, Bangalore July-2008 Report.

Yadagiri K. (1996), Rural Poor and a Challenging Task of DWCRA: A Study of Women in Andhra Pradesh. *Journal of Southern Economist*, Vol. 35(5), pp. 5-8.

Index

M

N

O

P

R

❑❑❑